SIMPLE

TO

SENSATIONAL

For my mother and father. Without your support I would not be where I am today.
And to my godchildren Paloma and Oscar.

First published in Great Britain by Simon & Schuster UK Ltd. 2009
A CBS Company

Copyright © Jun Tanaka

Simon & Schuster UK Ltd
1st Floor, 222 Gray's Inn Road, London WC2B 6AH

1 3 5 7 9 10 8 6 4 2

Design: Two Associates
Photography: Steve Lee
Styling: Jo Harris
Managing Editor: Paula Borton

Printed and bound in China

SIMPLE
TO
SENSATIONAL

PHOTOGRAPHY BY STEVE LEE

JUN TANAKA

SIMON &
SCHUSTER

LONDON • NEW YORK • SYDNEY • TORONTO

Contents

As far back as I can remember food has always been a passion. Growing up, the family dinner was the highlight of my day. My mother – a fantastic cook – would regularly read cookbooks and try out new recipes, so dinner was always a treat. I remember being especially excited when we had guests around for dinner, as she would go out of her way to create something special. The preparation started two days before, the kitchen littered with well-thumbed cookbooks, pots and pans, stewing and rattling on the stove. As the fridge began to overflow with the dishes, neatly organized into individual bowls, I would loiter in the kitchen and dip my fingers into every single one to the annoyance of my mother. Even as a child there was nothing I wouldn't eat.

Loving food so much, it seemed completely natural for me to become a chef, so with the guidance of my father I started my career at the age of 19. Over the next 10 years I was fortunate enough to work with some of the country's top chefs. To this day I vividly remember my first day as a chef, tentatively walking into Le Gavroche. The mixture of nerves and excitement I felt as I set foot in the kitchen and the array of smells and sounds will always stay with me. Even after 18 years of cooking professionally, I still feel that sense of excitement when I'm surrounded by food.

Being a chef is a large part of who I am. I feel truly lucky to have found a profession that I'm so passionate about. It's a feeling that through this book I want to share with you.

Cooking at home is a world apart from cooking in a professional kitchen. You don't have the equipment, manpower or access to some of the specialist ingredients. Nevertheless, there are certain simple techniques and ideas that you can utilize in your own home and I'm going to show you some of them.

Simple to Sensational is a book for beginners and for the more adventurous cook. I have written a collection of simple tasty recipes, from a fish pie to steak and chips using ingredients that are easily accessible. These are recipes that any novice can cook. For each simple recipe there is a more refined version, showing you that with a few easy techniques or by simply changing or adding a few key ingredients you can transform a simple dish into something sensational. In some recipes it could be as easy as presenting the dish differently, or in the case of a classic Bolognaise I have substituted the beef mince for venison, added a splash of red wine and cooked it in a low oven for two hours to make an unbelievably flavoursome sauce!

Try the simple recipes for your everyday use and once you've got the hang of them it's only a few small, easy steps to spectacular dinner party dishes. I hope you share my sense of excitement when you try these recipes and that your time in the kitchen will stimulate your imagination as well as your tastebuds.

JT

Handy kitchen equipment

Professional cooks love kitchen gadgets and I'm no exception. This is stuff I find really useful.

Muslin or cheesecloth
You can buy this in a fabric store. It's a white, finely woven cloth that is very handy for straining sauces.

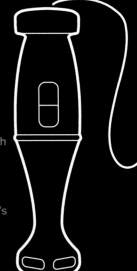

Squeezy bottles
I must have about 100 in my kitchen. They're very useful for storing cold sauces and vinaigrettes and using a bottle makes dressing a plate much easier.

Blender
I'm pretty sure that you have one of these, but I'm including it anyway because it really is an essential piece of equipment.

Pestle and mortar
No kitchen should be without one. It's great for spices and herbs. Always buy the largest one.

Non stick crêpe pan
These are not only good for making crêpes but also for cooking fish.

Hand blender
This does pretty much the same job as a blender but you can use it for smaller quantities of liquid. It's also useful for frothing sauces.

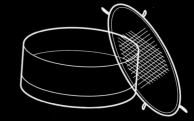

Steamer
You probably have this
as well. If you don't, buy
one in stainless steel.
You'll need it to smoke
duck breasts (page 49).

Japanese mandolin
In my kitchen it's
constantly used. It's the
best way to thinly slice
vegetables – just be
careful of your fingers!

Drum sieve
Use to sieve baked potatoes
when making mash or gnocchi.

Ramekins
You will need small ones, around
7 cm in diameter and 6 cm high.

Piping bags
Always buy the
disposable ones, as it's a
more hygienic.

Speed peeler
It does what it says and
makes peeling
vegetables a lot quicker.

cutters
buy a set of plastic
in all different sizes.

Melon-baller
This is the best way
to remove the seeds
from whole pears
(page 156–157).

Pastry brush
It's just handy to
have one.

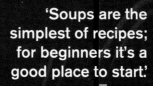

'Soups are the
simplest of recipes;
for beginners it's a
good place to start.'
Jun

soups

'simple'

'Light, elegant and bursting with flavour.'

'sensational'

'simple'

Creamy butternut squash soup

When you're shopping for butternut squash, choose ones that are golden in colour with no hint of green. These will have a deeper flavour. Change the butternut squash to pumpkin, celeriac, parsnips or carrots for a tasty variation.

Serves 6

15 g unsalted butter

1 onion, finely chopped

1 garlic clove, finely chopped

1 medium butternut squash (around 800 g), peeled, de-seeded and cut into 3 cm chunks

salt and freshly ground black pepper

800 ml chicken stock (see Tip on page 26)

80 g crème fraîche, plus extra for serving

1 Melt the butter in a large lidded pan. Add the onion and garlic and cook gently for 5 minutes. Add the butternut squash, season and cover with a lid. Sweat for 10 minutes, stirring occasionally to prevent the squash from burning.

2 Add the chicken stock, bring to the boil and simmer for 20 minutes. Finally, add the crème fraîche and bring to the boil. Remove from the heat and whizz in a blender until smooth. Reheat gently, adding more seasoning to taste if necessary.

3 Serve in warmed bowls with a dollop of crème fraîche on top of each serving.

Tip

When you're making the soup, it's important to cook and soften the butternut squash before adding the stock. This will give it a sweeter and nuttier flavour.

Variation

This soup is also fantastic with pieces of crispy bacon scattered on top.

SIMPLE

'sensational'

Butternut squash soup, caramelised scallops and toasted pumpkin seeds

When choosing scallops, always try and buy the hand-dived ones rather than the dredged. The latter tend to be gritty and the quality is not as good. Just ask your fishmonger. Scallops and butternut squash both have a natural soft sweetness that combine perfectly together. I've added the curry powder to contrast with the sweetness and the pumpkin seeds for the texture.

Serves 4

1 Creamy Butternut Squash Soup
    recipe (previous page), but with
    1 teaspoon mild curry powder
12 hand-dived scallops
salt and freshly ground black pepper
2 tablespoons light olive oil
15 g unsalted butter
15 g pumpkin seeds
juice of ½ lemon
red amaranth or chervil or tarragon
    leaves, to garnish

1 Prepare the Creamy Butternut Squash Soup, but this time add 1 teaspoon curry powder with the butternut squash.

2 Season the scallops. Heat the olive oil in a frying pan. Wait until the oil is very hot, then add the scallops. Cook for 1 minute then flip over and add the butter and pumpkin seeds. Cook for a further 1 minute, then add a squeeze of lemon juice.

3 To serve, pour the soup into warmed bowls, place 3 scallops on the top of each and then spoon over the pumpkin seeds with the butter left in the pan. For a pretty garnish, use some red amaranth, if you wish

Variation
To make a vegetarian version, switch the chicken stock for vegetable stock, remove the scallops and simply serve with croûtons and crumbled goat's cheese or Parmesan shavings.

see picture overleaf

Scallops and butternut
squash have a natural soft
sweetness that combine
perfectly together.

'sensational'

'simple'

Spring pea and mint soup

The great thing about this soup is that you can make it all year round because you use frozen peas. I do think that peas are the only vegetables that taste better frozen than fresh.

Serves 6

800 ml chicken or vegetable stock (see Tip on page 26)

500 g frozen peas

80 g crème fraîche

½ bunch fresh mint

salt and freshly ground black pepper

1 Bring the stock to the boil in a pan and add the peas. Cook for 1 minute, then add the crème fraîche. Remove from the heat and whizz in the blender with the mint leaves until smooth. Pour through a sieve to remove any lumps.

2 Reheat gently, season to taste and serve in warmed bowls.

Tip

If you're not serving this soup immediately, place the pan containing the soup in a larger pan filled with ice and water. This will chill the soup quickly and help it retain its green colour. You can also serve this soup chilled, but if you want to do that, use vegetable stock instead of chicken.

SIMPLE

'sensational'

Pea soup with mint froth

Frothy soups and sauces are used in professional kitchens to add lightness and movement to dishes. It's essentially more about presentation than flavour, but when combined with soups of thicker consistency, it's a great way to add two flavours together. In this case you get a burst of mint followed by the flavour of the peas.

Serves 6

1 Spring Pea and Mint Soup recipe (previous page), but without the mint

½ bunch fresh mint

2 tablespoons olive oil

1 tablespoon caster sugar

200 ml semi-skimmed milk

25 g unsalted butter

1 Make the Spring Pea and Mint Soup, but leave out the mint. Keep warm.

2 Preheat the oven to the lowest setting, Gas Mark ¼/110°C. Pick 12 nice mint leaves. Cover a flat plate in cling film, lightly oil and carefully lay the mint leaves on to the plate. Drizzle a little more olive oil on top and cover the leaves with another layer of cling film. Place in the microwave for 2 minutes on the lowest power. Take out and peel off the top layer of cling film. Put the plate in the oven for 20 minutes or until the leaves become dried.

3 Pour the milk into a pan and bring to the boil. Take off the heat and add the remaining mint leaves and the sugar. Leave to infuse for 30 minutes. Strain the milk through a sieve into a pan.

4 To serve, pour the soup into warmed bowls. Gently warm (but do not boil) the mint-infused milk, add the butter, let it melt, then froth with a hand blender. Spoon the froth onto the soup and garnish with the dried mint leaves.

Tip
Try infusing the milk with other flavours like garlic or toasted almonds. Add a pinch of salt to bring out the flavours.

'simple'

'Blending and sieving the fish soup
makes for a velvety consistency.'

'sensational'

'simple'

Onion, thyme and garlic soup

Here's a chef's tip. Whenever you're cooking onions, always cook them on a gentle heat and keep them covered with a lid. By doing this they will sweat gently and their natural sugars will be released, resulting in a sweeter flavour.

Serves 4

25 g unsalted butter

4 medium onions, finely sliced

6 garlic cloves, sliced

salt and freshly ground black pepper

1 large potato, peeled and sliced

1 tablespoon fresh thyme leaves

1 litre chicken or vegetable stock

50 g crème fraîche

1 Melt the butter in a large saucepan. Add the onions and garlic, season and cover. Gently sweat for 15 minutes, occasionally stirring to prevent everything from catching on the bottom.

2 Add the potato, thyme and stock. Simmer for 15 minutes or until the potatoes are soft, then add the crème fraîche. Whizz in a blender until smooth, check the seasoning, adding more if necessary, and serve.

Tip

A good stock is essential for making great-tasting soups. The best thing is to make your own, but I appreciate most people just don't have the time, so the next best thing is to buy fresh liquid stocks, which are available in the supermarkets. These have less salt than stock cubes and give soups, sauces and stews a richer consistency.

SIMPLE

'sensational'

Onion and thyme soup with onion bhajis

At Pearl, I usually serve a soup as an appetizer. But whatever soup it is, we always garnish it with something that enhances the flavour and presentation and adds contrast in taste and texture. In this instance I've added onion bhajis. The spices and crispy texture add an exciting contrast to the creamy onion soup.

Serves 6

1 Onion, Thyme and Garlic Soup
   recipe (previous page)
sunflower oil, for frying

For the onion bhajis

2 red onions, halved and finely sliced
1 red chilli, de-seeded and finely
   chopped
1 cm fresh ginger, peeled and grated
½ teaspoon cumin seeds, crushed
½ teaspoon mild curry powder
1 garlic clove, crushed
salt and freshly ground black pepper
50 g tempura flour or cornflour

1 Make the Onion, Thyme and Garlic Soup.

2 Place the red onions in a bowl. Add the chilli, ginger, cumin, curry powder, garlic and seasoning and leave for 30 minutes.

3 Using your hands, mix the tempura flour into the onion mixture. Shape into six balls.

4 Half fill a saucepan with oil and heat until a tiny piece of the mixture sizzles when dropped into the oil. If you have a deep fat fryer, heat to 170ºC. Deep fry the bhajis for 4 minutes until crisp and golden brown. Serve on the side with the soup.

Tip
Try substituting the onions in the soup base with three finely sliced leeks, and replace the chicken stock with vegetable stock. Use deep-fried shredded leeks (see page 93) instead of the onion bhajis and serve chilled for a delicious leek and potato soup.

sensational

'simple'

Smoked haddock chowder

When you make this recipe, it's best to use undyed smoked haddock. Serve with crusty bread to make a filling meal.

SIMPLE

Serves 6
500 g undyed smoked haddock
500 ml semi-skimmed milk
1 bay leaf
a sprig of fresh thyme
20 g unsalted butter
1 leek, finely chopped
1 garlic clove, crushed
1 teaspoon mild curry powder
a pinch of saffron threads
1 large potato, peeled and cut into
   1 cm cubes
50 ml whisky
300 ml chicken stock (see Tip on
   page 26)
80 g sweetcorn
100 ml double cream
salt and freshly ground black pepper
juice of ½ lemon
crusty bread, to serve

1 Skin the haddock and cut into chunks, place in a pan, cover with the milk and add the bay leaf and thyme. Bring to a simmer, take off the heat, cover and leave to infuse for 20 minutes.

2 In a separate pan, melt the butter, add the leek and cook gently for 3 minutes. Add the garlic, spices and potato, cook for another minute, then add the whisky and reduce for 1 minute. Finally add the chicken stock and simmer for 10 minutes.

3 Remove the thyme and bay leaf from the infused milk, and add the milk and fish to the soup. Add the sweetcorn, simmer for 5 minutes then add the double cream and bring to the boil. Check the seasoning, squeeze in some lemon juice and serve in warmed bowls with crusty bread.

Tip
Saffron is expensive, so as an alternative try using a teaspoon of ground turmeric.

Variation
To change this chowder into a beautiful fish stew, simply add a handful of fresh peas and 250 g of salmon, monkfish or cod cut into bite-sized pieces 5 minutes before the end. You can also use the stew as a filling for a delicious fish pie.

'sensational'

Smoked haddock soup, poached quail eggs and watercress dressing

If quail eggs are too fiddly, just serve with a poached hen's egg. The watercress adds a pleasant pepperiness to the dish.

Serves 6

1 Smoked Haddock Chowder recipe
   (previous page)
100 ml white wine vinegar
12 quail eggs
½ bunch watercress
100 ml olive oil
salt and freshly ground black pepper
juice of ½ lemon

1 Make the Smoked Haddock Chowder. When cooked, pick out about a quarter of the smoked haddock, separate into flakes and keep to one side. Pour the rest of the chowder into a blender and whizz until smooth. Pour through a sieve, squeezing the bits with the back of a ladle to extract as much juice as possible. Pour back into a saucepan and keep warm.

2 Pour the white wine vinegar into a bowl and carefully break the eggs into it. Leave for 5 minutes; the vinegar will start to cook the outside of the quail eggs so when they are poached they will form a perfect oval shape.

3 Bring a pan of water to the boil, add the eggs and vinegar and cook for 1½ minutes. Remove the eggs.

4 Whizz the watercress and olive oil in a blender, season and add a squeeze of lemon juice.

5 To serve, place a few haddock flakes into each bowl and top each with 2 eggs. Ladle over the soup and finish with a swirl of watercress dressing.

Variation
When you're making the watercress dressing, add a tablespoon of grated Parmesan cheese, a tablespoon of toasted pine nuts and a garlic clove. This makes an alternative to classic basil pesto. Use in the same way.

sensational

Adding pesto before serving makes this minestrone fresher and more vibrant.

'sensational'

'Salads can be so much more than green leaves and sliced cucumber. If you want to be adventurous in the kitchen, but still feel a little unsure of your skills, making a salad can be simple and satisfying.'

Jun

salads

'simple'

Charred pepper and tomato salad with grilled ciabatta

This is my version of a classic Italian dish, Panzanella, which means bread salad.

Serves 4

2 yellow peppers

2 red peppers

100 ml light olive oil, plus extra for the ciabatta

1 garlic clove

a sprig of fresh thyme

1 teaspoon caster sugar

salt and freshly ground black pepper

30 ml good quality red wine vinegar, preferably cabernet sauvignon

4 ripe plum tomatoes

100 g pitted black olives

20 g capers

8 anchovy fillets, preferably in vinegar

½ bunch fresh basil, torn

4 slices ciabatta, ½ cm thick each

1 Find a bowl large enough to fit all the peppers and fill with cold water. Using metal tongs, place each pepper straight on to the naked flame of a gas ring. Blacken the skin all over, turning the peppers for about 4–5 minutes. Place in the bowl of water.

2 Rub the peppers with your hands to remove the blackened skin. Don't worry if there's some left, a small amount will add to the flavour. Cut the peppers in half, remove the seeds and core and cut into 1 cm strips lengthways.

3 Heat the olive oil in a frying pan and gently cook the pepper strips for 2–3 minutes. Add the garlic, thyme and sugar. Season. Cook for a further minute, add the vinegar and remove to a bowl.

4 Bring a pan of water to the boil. Using a small knife, remove the eyes of the tomatoes where they were attached to the stalks and cut a cross in the skin at the opposite end. Plunge the tomatoes into the boiling water for 10 seconds, then remove and put straight into iced water. Peel, quarter and de-seed the tomatoes. Cut the quarters in half lengthways and add them to the peppers.

5 Add the olives, capers, anchovies and torn basil to the peppers and tomatoes. Mix well and remove the garlic and thyme.

6 Lightly oil the ciabatta slices and place them on a hot griddle for 30 seconds on each side.

7 To serve, place a slice of ciabatta on each plate and spoon over the salad.

see picture overleaf

'sensational'

Grilled sardine salad with peppers, tomato and basil dressing

I came up with this dish while on holiday in Italy, sitting on a terrace having lunch of plump barbecued sardines, a proper tomato salad and crunchy grilled ciabatta. It was fresh, simple and delicious. Ask your fishmonger to prepare the sardines for you. The smell of freshly grilled sardines always reminds me of being on holiday. Perhaps that's why I like them so much.

Serves 4

1 x Charred Pepper and Tomato Salad with Grilled Ciabatta recipe (previous page), but without the basil

1 bunch fresh basil

100 ml extra virgin olive oil, plus extra for oiling

salt and freshly ground black pepper

4 butterflied sardines

Tip

To cook the peppers in the oven, cut them in half and remove the seeds. Place on a baking tray skin side down and drizzle with olive oil. Season and roast at Gas Mark 4/180°C for 10 minutes. Remove, turn the peppers over and cook for a further 5 minutes. Remove from the oven and place in a bowl. Cover with cling film and leave for 10 minutes. When cooled, remove the skin and cut the flesh into strips. They do not need to be fried in the pan.

1 Make the Charred Pepper and Tomato Salad to the end of step 5, but don't use the basil. Keep the untoasted ciabatta slices to one side for now.

2 Place the bunch of basil leaves and olive oil in a blender and whizz to obtain a bright green oil. Season lightly.

3 Place the sardines on a lightly oiled baking tray, season and place under a hot grill for 3–4 minutes

4 This next part is purely for presentation, but it's worth having a go because it's so easy to do. Fold a kitchen cloth in half and lay a full wine bottle on its side on top (the cloth will prevent the bottle from moving). Lightly oil the ciabatta and griddle as in the Charred Pepper and Tomato Salad recipe, but as soon as both sides are done, place the slice of bread across the wine bottle and press the ends down gently to obtain a curved shape. Keep each slice in place for 10 seconds.

5 To serve, spoon the basil oil in a circle on each plate, place a slice of ciabatta in the centre, spoon on some of the pepper salad and finally top with a sardine.

sensational

'simple'

Grilled ciabatta gives this simple salad real crunch – a delicious contrast with the luscious peppers and tomatoes.

'simple'

'It's fun to transform this simple Nicoise salad
by separating the elements on the plate. This version
uses seared fresh tuna and quail eggs.'

'sensational'

'simple'

Fennel, blood orange and pomegranate salad

This is a refreshing salad of contrasting tastes and textures – the sweet softness of the blood oranges, the crunchiness of the fennel and the bitterness of the chicory. I think that's why it works so well.

Serves 4
4 blood oranges or pink grapefruit
2 fennel bulbs
2 pomegranates
2 red chicory
juice of 1 lemon
50 ml extra virgin olive oil
salt and freshly ground black pepper

1 Top and tail the oranges and, using a small sharp knife, cut off the skin and pith. Segment the oranges into a bowl and squeeze in any juice from the skin.

2 Cut the fennel bulbs into quarters lengthways, trim off the roots and peel away the outer layers, which can be quite tough. Cut the quarters into fine strips and add to the orange segments. Keep the herby tops.

3 To remove the seeds from the pomegranates, cut the fruit in half, hold the pomegranate cut-face down over the bowl and, holding a rolling pin with the other hand, gently tap the pomegranate to dislodge the seeds. Remove any pith that falls into the bowl.

4 Cut off the roots of the chicory and separate into leaves. Cut the leaves in half lengthways and add to the salad.

5 Squeeze in the lemon juice, add the olive oil and season to taste. Serve immediately, garnished with the herby fennel tops.

'sensational'

Mackerel salad with fennel, blood orange and pomegranate vinaigrette

Mackerel has to be one of my favourite fish. It's great value, hassle-free to cook and prepare (no scales) and also has a fantastic flavour. What more could you ask for?

Serves 4

1 Fennel, Blood Orange and Pomegranate Salad recipe (previous page)
4 additional pomegranates
juice of ½ lemon
50 ml extra virgin olive oil, plus a little extra for the mackerel
4 mackerel fillets
salt and freshly ground black pepper

1 Make the Fennel, Blood Orange and Pomegranate Salad, reserving the fennel tops.

2 Remove the seeds from the additional pomegranates, place in a blender and whizz for 30 seconds. Strain through a sieve and pour into a pan. Heat and reduce by half, which should take about 10 minutes. Whisk in the lemon juice and olive oil.

3 Cut the mackerel fillets in half lengthways, removing the bones running down the middle of the fillets. Lightly season and oil. Place on a hot griddle skin-side down for 2 minutes, then flip over and cook for a further minute.

4 To serve, spoon the salad into the centre of a plate, drizzle the pomegranate vinaigrette around the salad into the centre of a plate, criss-cross the mackerel fillets on top and finally garnish with the fennel tops.

Tip
Instead of mackerel, you could try using salmon or seabass. The pomegranate vinaigrette also makes a tasty marinade for steaks.

'simple'

Baby vegetable and almond salad with lemon and honey dressing

You can add fresh peas and broad beans to this. When they're around, try adding a handful of fresh morel mushrooms too. The season's really short, but they will take this salad to a whole new level. You should be able to buy lemon oil in most supermarkets.

Serves 4

8 new potatoes, peeled

salt

4 baby fennel bulbs

12 baby carrots, scraped clean

8 baby leeks, trimmed

8 asparagus spears, peeled and
cut in half

40 g whole almonds

½ bunch radish, finely sliced,
to garnish

For the lemon and honey dressing

1 tablespoon runny honey

juice of 2 lemons

50 ml lemon oil

100 ml extra virgin olive oil

salt and freshly ground black pepper

1 To make the lemon and honey dressing, put the honey in a bowl and add the lemon juice. Slowly whisk in the oils and season to taste.

2 Preheat the oven to Gas Mark 4/180°C.

3 Place the potatoes in a pan and cover with cold water, season with salt and simmer for 15 minutes or until cooked. Remove from the heat and place under cold running water.

4 For the next part you're going to need a timer. Place a large pan of water on to boil and season with salt. Once boiling, set the timer for 8 minutes. First put the fennel in the water. After 2 minutes, add the baby carrots, then 2 minutes after that the baby leeks. Add the asparagus 2 minutes later and leave all the vegetables to cook for the final 2 minutes. Drain and place in iced water.

5 Place the almonds on a baking tray and roast in the oven for 4 minutes.

6 Once the vegetables are cold, pat off any excess water, cut the carrots, leeks and fennel in half and place in a bowl with the asparagus. Slice the potatoes and add to the rest of the vegetables. Finally add the almonds and dress everything with 4 tablespoons of lemon and honey dressing.

7 Serve in a bowl garnished with the radishes.

SIMPLE

'sensational'

Crunchy iced vegetable salad with candied almonds

Be careful with your fingers when you make this salad and dress it right at the last minute. Keeping the vegetables on ice makes them curl beautifully and become ultra crunchy.

Serves 4

8 new potatoes, peeled
salt
8 baby leeks, trimmed
40 g caster sugar
40 g whole almonds
iced water
8 asparagus spears
12 baby carrots, scraped clean
½ bunch radish
4 baby fennel bulbs
1 Lemon and Honey Dressing recipe (previous page)

1 Cook the new potatoes as in step 3 of the recipe on the previous page. Cook the leeks in salted boiling water for 4 minutes.

2 Place the caster sugar in a pan, add a tablespoon of water and heat. Wait until the sugar turns a golden colour, then add the almonds. Coat the nuts in the caramel for 1 minute and then place on a tray lined with baking parchment.

3 Fill a large bowl with iced water. Remove the hard roots of the asparagus, lay the spears flat on a chopping board and, using a speed peeler (see page 9), peel ribbons of asparagus. Place the shavings in the iced water. Repeat the process with the carrots.

4 Finely slice the radish and fennel bulbs carefully on a Japanese mandolin (see page 9) and add to the iced water. Leave in the ice for 1 hour.

5 Slice the cooked potatoes into 2 cm thick pieces, cut the baby leeks in half, place in a bowl and dress with 3 tablespoons of lemon dressing.

6 Place the caramel almonds between two sheets of cling film and crush using a rolling pin, keeping the fragments quite coarse.

7 Drain the iced vegetables, dry well, place in a separate bowl and dress with 4 tablespoons of lemon dressing. Once the vegetables are dressed, serve immediately, otherwise they will become limp. To serve, lay six pieces of potato in the centre of a plate, add four pieces of baby leeks, a handful of the iced vegetables and finally sprinkle the almonds on top and around.

'simple'

Beetroot, goat's cheese and walnut salad

Beetroot and goat's cheese – what a fantastic combination! Like steak and chips or strawberries and cream, they are ingredients that are just meant to be eaten together. This salad is one of the easiest I know; it's just a matter of chopping everything up and mixing it in a bowl. But the result is amazing! Precooked beetroot can be bought vacuum-packed in its own juice from most supermarkets.

Serves 4

500 g precooked beetroot in its own juice, cut into 1.5 cm cubes

2 Granny Smith apples, cored and cut into 1.5 cm cubes

½ red onion, finely chopped

50 g walnuts

2 tablespoons runny honey

50 ml cabernet sauvignon vinegar or another good quality red wine vinegar

100 ml extra virgin olive oil

a handful rocket leaves

salt and freshly ground black pepper

100 g goat's cheese

1 Preheat the oven to Gas Mark 3/160°C

2 Place the beetroot and apples in a bowl. Add the red onion.

3 Place the walnuts on a baking tray and roast in the oven for 3–4 minutes. Remove and add to the salad.

4 Add the honey, vinegar, olive oil and rocket. Season and mix well. Finally crumble the goat's cheese into the salad. Gently mix through and serve.

SIMPLE

'sensational'

Smoked duck, beetroot and apple salad with crispy goat's cheese

If you're feeling adventurous you can smoke your own duck breasts – it's pretty simple to do. Just take a steamer (see page 9), line the bottom with tin foil, add 4–5 tablespoons of fresh tea leaves (Earl Grey or Lapsang Souchong work best), put the top half and lid back on and place on the heat. Once the tea is smoking, place the duck breasts in the steamer, cover with the lid and smoke for 3–4 minutes. Make sure you keep the windows open!

Serves 4

1 Beetroot, Goat's Cheese and Walnut
   Salad recipe (previous page), but
   without the goat's cheese
100 g goat's cheese
30 g plain flour
2 medium free range eggs
50 g Panko (Japanese breadcrumbs)
   or normal breadcrumbs
sunflower or groundnut oil, for frying
1 smoked duck breast

1 Make the Beetroot, Goat's Cheese and Walnut Salad, but don't add the goat's cheese.

2 Crumble the goat's cheese into a bowl. Take small amounts of cheese into the palm of your hand and roll into balls about the size of a coin, putting on a plate. Once all the cheese is used, place in the freezer to harden for 20 minutes.

3 Take three small plates or bowls. Place the flour in one, break and whisk the eggs into another and put the breadcrumbs in the third.

4 Once the goat's cheese has hardened, remove from the freezer and roll in the flour, then the eggs and finally the breadcrumbs. Coat in the eggs and breadcrumbs a second time to prevent the cheese from seeping out when cooked.

5 Half fill a pan with oil and heat until hot enough that a pinch of breadcrumbs sizzles when dropped into the oil. Alternatively, heat a deep fat fryer to 180°C. Fry the goat's cheese for 2 minutes or until golden brown. Take out and drain on kitchen paper.

6 Slice the duck into wafer-thin slices.

7 To serve, spoon the salad on to plates, lay five slices of duck on top of each and top with the goat's cheese.

sensational

'simple'

Charred vegetable and couscous salad

Every time I have a barbecue, I'll make some variation of this salad. It makes a great accompaniment for grilled fish or meats and it's so simple to prepare. The trick is to get the quantity of water to couscous just right.

Serves 6

300 g couscous

100 ml extra virgin olive oil

1 garlic clove

a sprig of fresh thyme

½ chicken stock cube

salt

1 red pepper, de-seeded and cut into
   2 cm cubes

1 courgette, cut into 2 cm cubes

1 aubergine, cut into 2 cm cubes

8 asparagus spears, peeled and
   cut in half

75 ml red wine vinegar

½ bunch spring onions, finely
   chopped

a handful rocket leaves

½ bunch fresh basil, roughly
   shredded

1 Place the couscous in a bowl. Measure out 300 ml of water, place in a saucepan and add 50 ml of olive oil, the garlic, thyme and stock cube. Season with salt. As soon as the water boils, remove from the heat and pour it over the couscous. Mix well and cover in cling film. Leave to steam for 20 minutes.

2 Place the pepper, courgette, aubergine and asparagus in a large bowl. Season, add 50 ml of olive oil and cook for 8–10 minutes on a hot griddle, moving them round occasionally. Do not pile the vegetables on top of each other – if they don't all fit, cook in batches. Once all the vegetables are cooked, place back in the bowl. Add the red wine vinegar and spring onions.

3 Take the cling film off the bowl of couscous, remove the garlic and thyme and fluff the couscous up with a fork. Once all the grains are separated, add to the vegetables. Add the rocket and basil, check the seasoning and serve.

make it sensational

'sensational'

Vine ripened tomato stuffed with couscous salad

This makes an exciting summer starter, when tomatoes are at their best. To change the dish to a main course, simply stuff two fillets of seabass with the couscous salad, tie with string, drizzle with olive oil and bake in the oven. Delicious!

Serves 6

1 x Charred Vegetable and Couscous Salad recipe (previous page)

12 tomatoes on the vine

50 ml olive oil

50 ml balsamic vinegar

3 garlic cloves, finely sliced

a sprig of fresh thyme

a sprig of rosemary

1 Make the Charred Vegetable and Couscous Salad.

2 Bring a pan of water to the boil, criss-cross the bottom of the tomatoes. Fill a bowl with iced water. When the water is boiling, put the tomatoes in and count to 10 seconds, then plunge into the iced water. Peel using a small knife but be careful not to remove the stem. Cut the top of the tomatoes to form a lid and keep to one side. Using a spoon, scoop out all the seeds and flesh leaving an empty shell. Season the inside with salt and pepper, add a teaspoon of balsamic vinegar and a drizzle of olive oil

3 Fill the tomatoes with the couscous salad and place the lid back on top. Repeat with all the tomatoes and arrange them on a roasting tray. Drizzle over the remaining olive oil, scatter the garlic and herbs on top. Season the stuffed tomatoes and cook in the oven at Gas Mark 4/ 180°C for 10 minutes. Serve immediately.

sensational

stuff some vine-ripened tomatoes with the couscous for a brilliant side dish or starter

see pictures overleaf

'A great salad for barbecues.'

'simple'

'sensational'

'simple'

Warm salad of roasted root vegetables and watercress

Warm salads are a great way to start a meal during the winter months. This recipe will work with most winter vegetables. Try butternut squash, swede or celeriac – they will all be delicious. The horseradish dressing is also fantastic with roast beef. Precooked beetroot can be bought vacuum packed in its own juice from most supermarkets.

Serves 4

40 g walnuts

salt

50 g purple sprouting or tenderstem broccoli

2 carrots

2 parsnips

30 ml light olive oil

20 g butter

freshly ground black pepper

100 g precooked beetroot in own juice, cut into 2 cm cubes

2 tablespoons runny honey

1 bunch watercress

For the horseradish dressing

150 g crème fraîche

1 tablespoon Dijon mustard

2 tablespoons creamed horseradish

juice of ½ lemon

salt and freshly ground black pepper

1 Preheat the oven to Gas Mark 3/160°C.

2 To make the horseradish dressing, mix together the crème fraîche, mustard and horseradish in a bowl, squeeze in the lemon juice and season to taste.

3 Place the walnuts on a baking tray and roast in the oven for 4 minutes. Bring a pan of water to the boil, add a little salt and cook the broccoli for 2 minutes. Remove from the pan and plunge into iced water. Peel the carrots and parsnips and cut into eighths lengthways.

4 Heat the olive oil in a frying pan and cook the carrots and parsnips for 3 minutes until they start to colour. Add the butter, season and cook for a further 3 minutes. Add the beetroot, honey, walnuts and broccoli and warm through.

5 To serve, place the vegetables on a plate, garnish with the watercress and spoon the dressing over the top.

'sensational'

Honey-glazed root vegetable salad, walnut paste and horseradish crème fraîche

During autumn and winter this dish regularly features on my menu in the restaurant. I adapt the recipe depending on which vegetables are in season. I think this is a fantastic way of using the best produce of the moment. In professional kitchens, this honey and vinegar marinade is called a 'gastric'. Once made it will keep for weeks.

Serves 4

1 Warm Salad of Roasted Root Vegetables and Watercress recipe (previous page), but without the walnuts and honey

For the honey and vinegar marinade

200 ml red wine vinegar

200 g runny honey

a sprig of fresh thyme

1 garlic clove

For the walnut paste

100 g walnuts

50 ml extra virgin olive oil

½ garlic clove

salt and freshly ground black pepper

juice of ½ lemon

1 Preheat the oven to Gas Mark 3/160°C. Make the marinade. Place all the ingredients in a pan and slowly simmer until reduced by half. When cooked, remove the garlic and thyme and store in a plastic container.

2 To make the walnut paste, place the walnuts on a baking tray and roast in the oven for 4 minutes. Remove, place the walnuts on a clean kitchen cloth and rub off as much skin as possible. Whizz in a blender with the olive oil and garlic to make a smooth paste. Season and add the lemon juice.

3 Make the Warm Salad of Roasted Root Vegetables and Watercress, but just before the vegetables come out of the pan, coat them in 2 tablespoons of the marinade.

4 To serve, place two dollops of the walnut paste on a plate and smear across the plate using the back of a spoon. Carefully place the vegetables in a criss-cross fashion over the top. Garnish with a few nice watercress leaves and finally drizzle over the horseradish dressing.

Tip

The walnut paste and honey and vinegar marinade are what I would describe as homemade store cupboard ingredients – recipes that are quick and easy to make, keep for weeks, are versatile and make a big impact when added to recipes. Try a couple of tablespoons of the walnut paste added to warm pasta or a risotto. Just fantastic!

'Rice and pasta are essential store cupboard ingredients. By adding a few ingredients you can have a quick, hassle-free meal.'

Jun

rice&
pasta

'simple'

Fragrant herb risotto

The most important techniques to remember when making a risotto are sweating the onions in butter until they are soft and translucent, coating the rice in the butter and onions, always adding hot stock a little at a time and getting the consistency and texture of the rice just right.

Serves 2

20 g unsalted butter

½ onion, finely chopped

500 ml chicken or vegetable stock
(see Tip on page 26)

100 g risotto rice, preferably Carnaroli

50 ml white wine

salt and freshly ground black pepper

1 tablespoon mascarpone

juice of ½ lemon

1 tablespoon mixed chopped fresh
chives, basil and tarragon

1 tablespoon freshly grated
Parmesan

1 Melt the butter in a shallow pan, add the onion and cover with a lid. Cook on a gentle heat for 5 minutes. Pour the stock into a separate pan and bring to a simmer.

2 Add the rice to the onions and coat in the butter. Add the white wine, reduce for 2 minutes, season and add just enough hot stock to cover the rice. Cook on a gently simmer for approximately 10 minutes, adding a little more hot stock once the previous batch has been absorbed by the rice.

3 When the rice has softened but still has a slight bite, add the mascarpone and stir in, followed by the lemon juice, herbs and Parmesan. Check the seasoning and serve immediately.

Tip

There are three main types of risotto rice – Arborio, Vialone Nano and Carnaroli. I always use Carnaroli. It absorbs the most amount of liquid and doesn't break up easily.

SIMPLE

'sensational'

Smoked salmon and herb risotto with fried quail eggs

When you're buying smoked salmon for this recipe, try to get it unsliced. That way you can cut the salmon into cubes, which will give the risotto an interesting texture.

Serves 2

1 Fragrant Herb Risotto recipe (previous page)

60 g smoked salmon, cut into 2 cm cubes

20 ml vegetable oil

2 quail eggs

1 punnet mustard cress

1 Make the Fragrant Herb Risotto, adding the smoked salmon with the herbs and Parmesan.

2 Heat the vegetable oil in a small frying pan. Carefully crack in the quail eggs and fry until the white is set.

3 Serve the risotto in a bowl. Place the quail eggs on top and garnish with the mustard cress.

'simple'

Wild mushroom risotto

This is a classic but, in my opinion, still one of the best risottos around.

SIMPLE

Serves 2

20 g unsalted butter

½ onion, finely chopped

1 garlic clove, crushed

500 ml chicken stock (see Tip on
    page 26)

100 g risotto rice, preferably Carnaroli

50 ml white wine

2 tablespoons olive oil

100 g mixed wild mushrooms,
    cleaned and washed

salt and freshly ground black pepper

1 tablespoon mascarpone

1 heaped tablespoon freshly grated
    Parmesan

1 tablespoon chopped fresh flat leaf
    parsley

juice of ½ lemon

1 Melt the butter in a saucepan, add the onion and garlic, cover with a lid and cook for 5 minutes. Pour the chicken stock into a separate pan and bring to a simmer.

2 Add the rice to the onions and coat in the butter. Add the white wine, boil and reduce for 2 minutes. Add just enough hot stock to cover the rice.

3 Heat the olive oil in a separate frying pan and fry the mushrooms for 3 minutes until golden brown. Season and add to the rice. Cook the rice and mushrooms for 10 minutes, adding a little more stock once the previous batch has been absorbed by the rice.

4 When the rice has softened but still has a slight bite, add the mascarpone, Parmesan, parsley and lemon juice. Check the seasoning and serve.

make it sensational

'sensational'

Crisp wild mushroom risotto with mozzarella

This was invented as a way of using up leftover risotto from the night before. It is what the Italians call 'Arancina', which means 'orange' in reference to the shape of the risotto ball. It's absolutely delicious; the crisp outer coating, soft risotto and oozing mozzarella makes for a surprising dish.

Serves 4

1 Wild Mushroom Risotto recipe
   (previous page)
1 buffalo mozzarella
40 g plain flour
2 medium free range eggs
50 g Panko (Japanese breadcrumbs)
   or normal breadcrumbs
sunflower or groundnut oil, for frying
a handful rocket leaves
a handful Parmesan shavings
2 tablespoons balsamic vinegar
50 ml extra virgin olive oil

1 Make the Wild Mushroom Risotto. Pour into a large shallow dish, leave for 10 minutes to cool down, cover with cling film and place in the fridge for 2 hours or until firm.

2 Once the risotto is firm to touch, form into four balls using your hands. Keep rolling the risotto in the palm of your hands to achieve the right shape. Cut off four pieces from the mozzarella that are the size of a pound coin. Insert a finger into the centre of the balled risotto to make a hole and place a piece of the mozzarella inside. Reform the ball, completely encasing the mozzarella. Repeat with the other balls. Place on a plate and put back in the fridge for 1 hour to firm up.

3 When the risotto balls are set, take three plates or bowls. Put the flour on one, break and whisk the eggs into another and place the breadcrumbs on the third. Take the risotto balls out of the fridge, coat well in the flour, then in the eggs and finally in the breadcrumbs. Coat in the eggs and breadcrumbs a second time to give a double coating.

4 Half fill a pan with oil and heat until hot enough that a pinch of breadcrumbs sizzles when dropped into the oil. Alternatively, heat a deep fat fryer to 170°C. Deep fry the risotto balls for 5 minutes or until crisp and golden brown. Serve on a plate with the rocket and Parmesan shavings and dressed with the olive oil and balsamic vinegar.

Create crispy risotto balls stuffed with mozzarella (see step 2)

see pictures overleaf

'simple'

'These crispy balls, oozing with mozzarella, are a great way to use
up leftover risotto.'

'sensational'

'simple'

Fast pappardelle bolognaise

Spaghetti bolognaise was one of the first recipes I learnt to make – even before I started to cook professionally. In the restaurant, along with a curry, it's still one of the favourite dishes for staff dinner.

Serves 4
100 ml olive oil
½ onion, finely chopped
1 garlic clove, crushed
1 tablespoon tomato purée
350 g tinned tomatoes
1 teaspoon dried oregano
500 g minced beef
salt and freshly ground black pepper
200 g dried pappardelle
½ bunch fresh basil
a handful freshly grated Parmesan

1 Heat half the olive oil in a large pan and add the onion and garlic. Cover with a lid and cook on a gentle heat for 5 minutes. Add the tomato purée and cook for 2 minutes, then add the tinned tomatoes and oregano and bring to a simmer.

2 Heat the remaining olive oil in a separate frying pan and fry the mince for 5 minutes or until golden brown. Season and add to the simmering tomatoes. Add 100 ml water to the pan used to fry the mince and scrape all the bits off the bottom (these have loads of flavour). Add to the mince and simmer for 20 minutes.

3 Cook the pappardelle in boiling salted water for 8–10 minutes, then drain. To serve, add freshly torn basil to the mince and spoon the sauce over the pasta. Finish by sprinkling with the Parmesan.

SIMPLE

'sensational'

Pappardelle with venison bolognaise

Venison has a richer and stronger flavour than beef. Combine that with the red wine, spices and slow cooking and you have a bolognaise like you've never tasted before. If you can't find cracked black pepper, use crushed black peppercorns instead.

Serves 4

100 ml olive oil
½ onion, finely chopped
1 carrot, finely chopped
1 celery stick, finely chopped
1 garlic clove, crushed
1 tablespoon tomato purée
1 teaspoon cracked black pepper
3 juniper berries, crushed
200 g tinned tomatoes
300 ml beef stock
500 g venison mince
salt and freshly ground black pepper
250 ml red wine
200 g pappardelle
a handful freshly grated Parmesan

1 Preheat the oven to Gas Mark 4/180°C.

2 Heat half the olive oil in a large, lidded ovenproof pan and add the onion, carrot, celery and garlic. Cover with a lid and cook on a gentle heat for 5 minutes. Add the tomato purée, black pepper and juniper berries. Cook for a further 2 minutes, then add the tinned tomatoes and beef stock and bring to a simmer.

3 Heat the remaining olive oil in a separate frying pan and fry the venison mince on a high heat until golden brown. Season and add to the simmering tomatoes. Pour the red wine into the pan used to fry the mince and scrape all the bits off the bottom. Add to the mince. Cover with a lid and cook in the oven for 2½ hours.

4 Just before serving, cook the pappardelle in boiling salted water for 8–10 minutes. Drain and serve with a generous serving of venison bolognaise and a scattering of Parmesan.

✳ By simply replacing the beef mince with venison and cooking the bolognaise for longer, you will get a sauce that is deeper and richer in flavour.

sensational

**Frying gnocchi transforms
the taste and texture.**

'sensational'

'simple'

Simple rice pilaff

There's a little more butter than usual in this recipe but that's going to give it the wonderful flavour. Trust me it's worth it.

Serves 4

50 g unsalted butter

½ onion, finely chopped

1 garlic clove, crushed

200 g long grain rice

400 ml chicken stock (see Tip on page 26)

a sprig of fresh thyme

1 bay leaf

salt and freshly ground black pepper

1 Preheat the oven to Gas Mark 4/180°C.

2 Melt the butter in an ovenproof pan with a tight-fitting lid. Add the onion and garlic, cover and cook gently for 5 minutes. Add the rice and coat in the butter. Add the chicken stock, thyme, bay leaf and seasoning. Bring to a simmer, cover with the lid and cook in the oven for 20 minutes.

3 Take out of the oven and leave to sit for 10 minutes. Serve with a creamy chicken casserole or grilled fish.

Tip
As a simple alternative, try adding 2 tablespoons of freshly grated Parmesan, 1 tablespoon chopped chives and the juice of half a lemon.

SIMPLE

'sensational'

Chicken and prawn rice pilaff

This is my variation of the Spanish 'paella'. Normally short grain paella rice is used but it works equally well with long grain. If you love seafood, try adding live mussels, clams and squid with the king prawns. The best part of serving this dish is the moment you take the lid off when you're hit with wonderful aromas.

Serves 4

50 ml olive oil
4 free range chicken thighs
salt and freshly ground black pepper
½ onion, finely chopped
1 garlic clove, crushed
1 red pepper, de-seeded and finely
    chopped
½ green pepper, de-seeded and finely
    chopped
100 g chorizo, sliced
½ teaspoon ground turmeric
½ teaspoon smoked paprika
2 plum tomatoes, roughly chopped
50 g frozen peas
150 g long grain rice
100 ml white wine
200 ml chicken stock (see Tip on
    page 26)
8 peeled king prawns
lemon wedges, to serve

1 Preheat the oven to Gas Mark 4/180°C.

2 Heat the olive oil in a large ovenproof pan with a tight-fitting lid. Season the chicken thighs and add them to the pan. Cook for 5 minutes or until caramelised. Add the onion, garlic, peppers and chorizo and cook for a further 3 minutes. Add the turmeric, paprika, tomatoes, peas and rice, stir well, then add the white wine and reduce for 2 minutes. Add the chicken stock, season and bring to a simmer. Cover with the lid and place in the oven for 15 minutes.

3 Take out of the oven, add the prawns on top, cover and place back in the oven for a further 5 minutes. Once the pilaff is cooked, leave it to sit for 10 minutes. Serve with lemon wedges.

sensational

'simple'

Linguini with lightly spiced mussels

When cooking with any shellfish, it's vital that they are ultra fresh. To check, discard any with broken shells, then soak them in water for 1 hour (this will also remove the grit). If any are still open, throw them away. Finally after the shellfish is cooked, throw away the ones that are still closed.

Serves 4

50 ml olive oil

½ onion, finely chopped

1 garlic clove, crushed

1 leek, finely chopped

1 teaspoon curry powder

a pinch of saffron threads

300 g live mussels

300 g clams

200 ml white wine

150 ml double cream

1 bunch fresh chives, finely chopped

juice of ½ lemon

salt

200 g linguini

1 Heat the olive oil in a pan. Add the onion, garlic and leek and cook on a gentle heat for 3 minutes. Add the curry powder and saffron, cook for 1 minute, then add the mussels and clams followed by the white wine. Cover with a lid and cook for 6 minutes or until the shellfish open. Add the cream, bring to the boil and add the chives and a squeeze of lemon juice.

2 Bring a pan of salted water to the boil. Add the linguini and cook for 8–10 minutes. Drain in a colander and add to the mussels and clams. Mix well and serve.

'sensational'

Lasagne of mussels and clams with crispy squid

The squid adds an interesting texture to the dish. The spiced mussels and clams also make a delicious sauce for all grilled fish.

Serves 4

1 Linguini with Lightly Spiced Mussels recipe (previous page), but without the linguini
3 plum tomatoes
1 leek
salt
8 lasagne sheets
olive oil, for drizzling
100 g cleaned baby squid, cut into rings
1 tablespoon plain flour
sunflower or groundnut oil, for frying
1 teaspoon mild curry powder

1 Make the sauce for the Linguini with Lightly Spiced Mussels, but do not add the chives yet.

2 Place the sauce in a colander and drain into a clean pan. Reserve 12 mussels and 12 clams in the shells. Pick out the meat from the rest of the shellfish and discard the shells. Add the meat and the shellfish still in the shell back into the pan.

3 Peel and de-seed the tomatoes (see page 13, step 1, for how). Cut into 1 cm dice and add to the mussels and clams. Halve the leek lengthways, rinse, then cut into 1 cm dice. Cook in boiling salted water for 1 minute, drain in a colander and add to the mussels, clams and tomatoes.

4 Cook the lasagne sheets in boiling salted water for 8–10 minutes, then drain in a colander. Drizzle over a little olive oil to stop them from sticking together. Trim all the pasta sheets to obtain 10 cm squares and keep to one side.

5 Dip the squid rings in the flour. Half fill a pan with oil and heat until one of the rings sizzles when dropped into the oil. Alternatively, heat a deep fat fryer to 170°C. Deep fry the squid for 30 seconds or until crisp, drain on kitchen paper, sprinkle over the curry powder and season with salt.

6 To serve, gently warm the sauce and add the chives. Lay one sheet of pasta on the bottom of a bowl and spoon some of the mussels and clams into the centre. Lay another sheet on top and add more shellfish. Arrange the shellfish in the shell around the pasta, spoon over some sauce and finally scatter some of the deep fried squid on top.

see picture overleaf

Lasagne – but not as we know it…

'sensational'

'simple'

Penne with spinach, pine nuts and ricotta

When I'm in a rush and want a quick dinner, this is what I cook at home. It'll take you almost as long to read the recipe as it takes to cook the pasta – about 8 minutes.

Serves 4
50 g pine nuts
salt
300 g penne
50 ml olive oil
½ onion, finely chopped
1 garlic clove, crushed
250 g spinach, washed and chopped
200 g ricotta
20 g freshly grated Parmesan
freshly ground black pepper

1 Place the pine nuts in a dry frying pan and gently heat until they are toasted and golden brown. Keep to one side.

2 Bring a large pot of water to the boil, add salt and cook the pasta for 8–10 minutes. Drain and keep warm.

3 To make the sauce, heat the olive oil in a pan, add the onion and garlic, cover with a lid and cook on a gentle heat for 5 minutes. Add the pine nuts, spinach and ricotta. Once the ricotta has melted, add the penne and Parmesan, coat the pasta well, season with salt and pepper and serve.

SIMPLE

'sensational'

Cannelloni of spinach, pine nuts and ricotta with semi-dried tomatoes

The spinach and ricotta filling can be made the day before and kept in the fridge. Then its just a matter of putting everything together. The dried tomatoes will keep for a week covered in oil in a jar. They are a really useful store cupboard ingredient.

Serves 4

50 ml olive oil, for oiling

10 vine-ripened cherry tomatoes

2 garlic cloves, finely sliced

a sprig of fresh rosemary, finely chopped

salt and freshly ground black pepper

1 Penne with Spinach, Pine Nuts and Ricotta recipe (previous page), but without the penne

12 lasagne sheets

2 tablespoons freshly grated Parmesan

sunflower oil, for frying

1 bunch fresh basil, roughly shredded

1 Lightly oil a baking tray, cut the cherry tomatoes in half and place on the tray, cut side facing upwards. Place one slice of garlic on each tomato. Sprinkle over the chopped rosemary, season with salt and pepper and place in the oven at Gas Mark ¼/110°C for 2 hours.

2 Make the Penne with Spinach, Pine Nuts and Ricotta, but without the penne. Pour on to a tray and chill in the fridge. This is the cannelloni filling.

3 Bring a pan of water to the boil, season, add the lasagne sheets, cook for 3–4 minutes, drain and place in a bowl of cold water. Taking the pasta sheets one by one, trim them into 10 cm squares. Lightly oil the sheets to prevent them sticking. Working on a chopping board, take each pasta square and spoon a line of the filling along one side of the sheet. Roll to form a tube. Place on an oiled baking tray and repeat the process with all the squares, placing them on the tray in threes to make 12 tubes. Sprinkle the grated Parmesan over the cannelloni and place under a medium hot grill for 3–4 minutes or until golden brown.

4 Half fill a pan with oil and heat until hot, or heat a deep fat fryer to 170°C. Pick off the basil leaves and deep fry for 1 minute (be careful as they will spit). Remove with a slotted spoon and drain on kitchen paper. Season with salt.

5 To serve, carefully lift three cannelloni on to a plate using a spatula. Top with five dried tomatoes and garnish with the basil.

'Fresh fish is a must! Look for glistening eyes, crimson gills, firm flesh and the smell of the ocean.'
Jun

'simple'

Red mullet with crushed potatoes and fennel salad

Fennel and fish is a natural combination. Crushing potatoes is a great alternative to mash, but unlike mash it works better with waxy potatoes.

Serves 4
400 g new potatoes, peeled
salt
100 ml extra virgin olive oil
50 ml sherry vinegar
¼ bunch spring onions, chopped
freshly ground black pepper
2 fennel bulbs
juice of 1 lemon
a sprig of fresh dill, chopped
4 red mullet fillets
light olive oil, for baking tray

1 Place the potatoes in a pan, cover with cold water, add salt and simmer until cooked. Drain in a colander, add half the olive oil, sherry vinegar and spring onions and season. Crush with a fork and keep to one side.

2 To make the fennel salad, cut the fennel into quarters and cut out the root. Finely slice and place in a bowl, add the remaining olive oil, lemon juice, dill and season.

3 To cook the red mullet, place them skin side up on a lightly oiled baking tray, season and place under a hot grill for 6–8 minutes.

4 To serve, spoon the crushed potato on to a plate, top with a fillet of red mullet and place the fennel salad on the side.

Tip
The best way to tell when fish is perfectly cooked is with a cocktail stick. Insert the cocktail stick into the thickest part of the fish; if you feel a slight resistance it's not cooked. Couldn't be easier!

'sensational'

Red mullet coated in almonds with garlic crushed potatoes and fennel

Almonds and red mullet work beautifully together – the almonds give a wonderful texture to the fish.

Serves 4

1 Red Mullet with Crushed Potatoes and Fennel Salad recipe (previous page), but without the olive oil and sherry vinegar for the crushed potatoes
a sprig of fresh rosemary, chopped
50 g flaked toasted almonds
2 medium free range egg whites
light olive oil, for baking tray
For the garlic mayonnaise
1 garlic clove, crushed
juice of ½ lemon
a pinch of saffron threads
2 tablespoons good quality mayonnaise

1 To make the garlic mayonnaise, mix the garlic, lemon and saffron in a bowl. Add the mayonnaise and mix well.

2 Cook the new potatoes as described in the Red Mullet with Crushed Potatoes and Fennel Salad recipe, but without the olive oil and sherry vinegar. Crush with a fork, add the garlic mayonnaise and spring onions. Keep to one side.

3 Make the Fennel Salad.

4 To cook the red mullet, add the rosemary to the almonds and place on a plate. Pour the egg whites on to a separate plate and break up with a fork. Dip the red mullet fillets, skin side down into the egg white then into the almonds and press down. Carefully lift the fish on to an oiled baking tray and place skin side up (the almonds will have coated the skin). Place under a low to medium grill for 6–8 minutes.

5 To serve, spoon the potatoes on to a plate, top with the red mullet and serve with the fennel salad.

Tip
The egg white helps the almonds stick on to the fish without giving it an eggy flavour. Try an alternative coating of pistachios or sesame seeds.

Variation
Try mixing the garlic crushed potato with cubes of diced smoked salmon and cucumber to make a delicious potato salad.

see picture overleaf

81

Almonds and mullet work
brilliantly together – not
only in taste but texture too.

'sensational'

'simple'

Sea trout with Jersey Royals, asparagus and crème fraîche

This dish uses the very best of English spring produce – asparagus and Jersey Royal potatoes. Their seasons are short, so make the most of them when they're around.

Serves 4

400 g Jersey Royal potatoes, scrubbed clean

salt and freshly ground black pepper

12 asparagus spears

4 x 150 g sea trout fillets

light olive oil, for baking tray

25 g unsalted butter

For the crème fraîche sauce

4 tablespoons crème fraîche

½ shallot, finely chopped

10 drops Tabasco

½ garlic clove, crushed

a sprig of fresh dill, finely chopped

½ bunch chives, finely chopped

salt and freshly ground black pepper

1 To cook the Jersey Royal potatoes, place in a pan, cover with cold water, season and simmer for 15 minutes until cooked. Drain and keep to one side.

2 Trim away the woody ends of the asparagus about 2 cm from the bottom, then peel the ends. Bring a pan of water to the boil and cook in boiling salted water for 3–4 minutes. Remove, plunge into iced water, drain and add to the Jersey Royals.

3 Combine all the ingredients for the crème fraîche sauce together in a bowl and season to taste.

4 Place the sea trout fillets on an oiled baking tray, skin side up, season and place under a hot grill for 6–8 minutes.

5 To serve, melt the butter in a pan, add the Jersey Royals and asparagus, season and warm through. Place in a bowl, top with the sea trout and spoon on the crème fraîche sauce.

Tip

For a perfectly seasoned boiled potato, add 15 g of salt per litre of water. Try adding fresh mint, tarragon or thyme to the Jersey Royals when they're cooking.

SIMPLE

'sensational'

Cured sea trout poached in olive oil with Jersey Royals and asparagus

Curing fish before cooking is a wonderful way of enhancing their flavour. This cure recipe will work well with all fish. Poaching the sea trout in olive oil will also give it a 'melt in the mouth' texture.

Serves 4

1 Sea Trout with Jersey Royals, Asparagus and Crème Fraîche recipe (previous page)

For the cure

finely grated zest and juice of 1 orange

finely grated zest and juice of 1 lemon

300 g coarse sea salt

100 g caster sugar

1 teaspoon white peppercorns, crushed

1 teaspoon coriander seeds, crushed

For the poaching liquid

4 star anise

1 tablespoon fennel seeds

600 ml olive oil

1 To make the cure, combine all the ingredients in a glass bowl. Take 4 tablespoons of this marinade and coat the sea trout fillets all over. Leave for 15 minutes. Wash the fillets in cold water and then dry on kitchen paper. Set aside. The rest of the cure will keep for 2 weeks in a plastic container in the fridge.

2 To make the poaching liquid, add the star anise and fennel seeds to the olive oil, pour into a pan large enough to fit the fish and let infuse on a very low heat (not even simmering) for 30 minutes.

3 Cook the Jersey Royals and asparagus as in steps 1 and 2 of the Sea Trout with Jersey Royals, Asparagus and Crème Fraîche recipe. Prepare the crème fraîche sauce.

4 Heat the poaching liquid to no higher than 70°C, place the sea trout fillets in it and leave for 10 minutes. This poaching liquid can be used again and again and will keep very well.

5 To serve, place the potatoes and asparagus in a bowl, top with the fish and spoon on the crème fraîche sauce.

✳ Simple techniques like curing the sea trout and poaching in olive oil will enhance the flavour and texture of the fish.

Baked sea bass with mozzarella, olives and tomatoes

This is the easiest fish dish. It's just a matter of putting everything on a tray and baking it in the oven, but it's so tasty.

Serves 4
2 fennel bulbs
50 ml light olive oil, plus extra for
    baking tray
4 x 150 g sea bass fillets
1 buffalo mozzarella, sliced into four
300 g vine-ripened cherry tomatoes,
    halved
80 g pitted black olives
8 fresh basil leaves
25 ml balsamic vinegar
salt and freshly ground black pepper

1 Preheat the oven to Gas Mark 4/180°C.

2 Cut the fennel lengthways into 1 cm thick slices and place on an oiled baking tray. Put the sea bass fillets on top side by side.

3 Place a slice of mozzarella on each fillet. Scatter the tomato halves on the tray with the olives. Place two basil leaves on each fillet of sea bass. Drizzle over the extra olive oil and the balsamic vinegar. Season well.

4 Bake in the oven for 10 minutes. Serve immediately.

see picture overleaf

SIMPLE

'sensational'

Stuffed sea bass with tomato salsa

Stuffed fish is a great dinner party dish and it's pretty simple to do. Instead of mozzarella, try using sun-dried tomatoes. The tomato salsa is delicious by itself as a salad or as a side dish for roast lamb.

Serves 4

2 fennel bulbs

1 buffalo mozzarella

8 x 100 g sea bass fillets

2 tablespoons Pesto (see page 31)

salt and freshly ground black pepper

50 ml olive oil

For the tomato salsa

240 g vine-ripened cherry tomatoes,
    cut in half

80 g pitted black olives

20 g capers

½ red onion, finely chopped

4 anchovy fillets in vinegar, chopped

100 ml extra virgin olive oil

50 ml balsamic vinegar

salt and freshly ground black pepper

1 To make the tomato salsa, place all the ingredients for the salsa in a bowl, season and mix well.

2 Preheat the oven to Gas Mark 4/180°C.

3 Cut the fennel into 1 cm thick pieces and place on a baking tray. Slice the mozzarella into four pieces. Take four fillets of sea bass and place one slice of mozzarella on each one.

4 Spread half a tablespoon of pesto on the flesh of each of the other four fillets and place them pesto-side down on top of the sea bass with the mozzarella. Carefully lift the stuffed sea bass on to the fennel, season and drizzle with the olive oil. Bake in the oven for 15 minutes (test with a cocktail stick to ensure the fish is cooked; see Tip on page 80).

5 To serve, place the fennel and sea bass on a plate and spoon over the tomato salsa.

sensational

'simple'

"Bake this for just 10 minutes for the simplest and most delicious supper."

'simple'

Roast salmon with wild mushrooms and clams

The natural juice from clams and mussels makes an instant, delicious sauce for all fish. Just be careful how much salt you add – the juice is naturally salty. Salmon should always be served slightly underdone to prevent it from being too dry.

Serves 4

**50 ml light olive oil, plus an extra
  2 tablespoons**

1 shallot, finely chopped

1 garlic clove, crushed

500 g mixed wild mushrooms

a sprig of fresh thyme

salt and freshly ground black pepper

**600 g fresh clams, soaked for
  30 minutes in salted water**

150 ml white wine

2 tablespoons crème fraîche

juice of 1 lemon

½ bunch fresh chives, finely chopped

**4 x 150 g pieces salmon, skin
  removed**

25 g unsalted butter

1 Heat the 50 ml of olive oil in a pan and add the shallot and garlic. Cook for 2 minutes. Add the wild mushrooms and thyme, season and cook for a further 3 minutes. Add the clams and white wine, cover with a lid and cook for 3–4 minutes or until the clams open (discard any that remain closed). Add the crème fraîche, half the lemon juice and chives and stir. Keep warm.

2 Preheat the oven to Gas Mark 4/180°C.

3 Heat the 2 tablespoons of olive oil in a non-stick, ovenproof pan, season the salmon and cook for 2 minutes or until caramelised. Add the butter, flip the salmon over and bake in the oven for 5 minutes (the salmon should still be slightly underdone in the centre). Add a squeeze of lemon juice.

4 To serve, divide the mushrooms and clams into four bowls and top each one with a piece of salmon.

'sensational'

Baked salmon covered in garlic croûtons, clams and wild mushrooms

I learnt the trick of covering fish in croûtons from Nico Ladenis – a 3 Michelin Star chef. It's an interesting technique for adding crunchiness and looks amazing.

Serves 4

2 garlic cloves
50 g unsalted butter, melted
1 Roast Salmon with Wild Mushrooms
    and Clams recipe (previous page),
    but without the butter
2 medium free range egg whites
4 slices white bread
salt and freshly ground black pepper

1 Crush the garlic, add to the melted butter and infuse for 10 minutes. Brush a baking tray with some of the garlic-infused butter.

2 Cook the clams and mushrooms as in step 1 of the the Roast Salmon with Wild Mushrooms and Clams recipe and keep to one side.

3 Preheat the oven to Gas Mark 4/180°C.

4 To prepare the salmon, pour the egg whites on to a plate. Take a slice of white bread, cut off the crusts and cut into 2 cm squares. You should end up with a square of bread made up of about 16 smaller squares. Dip what was the skin side of the salmon into the egg white then carefully place on to the cut bread and press down gently.

5 Using a fish slice, carefully lift the piece of salmon covered with the croûtons and flip over on to the tray so it is bread-side up. Repeat with the other pieces of salmon. Season and place under a grill for 1 minute or until the bread turns golden. Spoon the remaining garlic butter over the fish and then place in the oven for 6 minutes.

6 To serve, pour the mushrooms and clams into a bowl and carefully place the salmon on top.

'simple'

Curried monkfish medallions with creamed leeks

This is fast fish food. It works equally well with scallops. Try adding shreds of deep-fried leeks (see next page) for texture and eye-catching appeal.

Serves 4
600 g monkfish loin
1 tablespoon mild curry powder
20 g plain flour
salt and freshly ground black pepper
1 tablespoon light olive oil
For the creamed leeks
2 leeks
25 g unsalted butter
1 garlic clove, crushed
100 ml double cream
salt and freshly ground black pepper

1 To make the creamed leeks, cut the leeks in quarters lengthways leaving the root intact and wash under running water. Finely chop. Heat the butter in a pan, then add the leeks and garlic. Season and cook for 5 minutes. Add the double cream and cook for a further 3 minutes. Keep warm.

2 Slice the monkfish into 2.5 cm thick pieces. Mix the curry powder and flour together on a plate and season. Dip one side of the monkfish pieces into the flour.

3 Heat a frying pan and add the olive oil. Add the monkfish, floured side down and cook for 2 minutes or until caramelised. Flip over and cook for a further 2 minutes.

4 To serve, spoon the creamed leeks on to plates and place several pieces of monkfish on top of each.

Monkfish poached in spiced red wine with creamed leeks

You would normally pair fish with white wine so it might seem unusual to use red wine in this dish but, trust me, it works. The acidity in the red wine acts in the same way as lemon juice and cuts through the richness of the fish. This will work with all meaty fish like turbot or brill. If you prefer not to deep fry the leeks, skip step 5.

Serves 4

4 x 150 g monkfish pieces
salt and freshly ground black pepper
25 g unsalted butter
1 Creamed Leeks recipe
  (previous page)
For the deep-fried leeks
400 ml vegetable oil
1 leek, finely shredded
1 tablespoon plain flour
For the poaching liquid
2 cinnamon sticks
3 star anise
1 tablespoon coriander seeds
1 tablespoon green cardamom pods
1 tablespoon black peppercorns
500 ml red wine
750 ml red port
1 bay leaf

1 To make the poaching liquid, gently toast the spices in a dry pan for 2 minutes. Pour the red wine and port into a pan and add the toasted spices and bay leaf. Bring to the boil then simmer for 30 minutes.

2 Season the monkfish and leave for 20 minutes to allow the seasoning to penetrate the fish. Then add to the poaching liquid and cook for 7–8 minutes (test whether it's cooked with a cocktail stick; see Tip on page 80).

3 Strain a ladleful of the poaching liquid into a small pan, add the butter and reduce until thick and glossy.

4 Make the Creamed Leeks.

5 For the deep-fried leeks, coat the leek in flour and shake off the excess. Heat the vegetable oil in a pan. Carefully place the leek in the oil and cook for 1 minute or until golden. Remove using a slotted spoon and drain on kitchen paper.

6 To serve, spoon some of the leeks into the centre of a plate, cut a piece of monkfish in half at an angle and place on top of the leeks. Drizzle the reduced sauce around. Top with deep-fried leeks.

Tip
To get the most out of spices, always lightly toast them first to release their flavours.

"White fish poached in red wine seems unusual, but trust me it works.

'sensational'

'simple'

Homely ocean pie

You can't beat a good fish pie. Try different combinations of fish but always keep the smoked haddock. You won't need any more than three varieties otherwise you'll lose their individual flavours.

Serves 6

600 g mixed salmon, cod and smoked
    haddock, cut into chunks

100 g frozen peas

salt and freshly ground black pepper

juice of ½ lemon

mixed green salad, to serve

For the mash

2 large Désirée potatoes

50 ml milk

50 g unsalted butter

salt and freshly ground black pepper

For the béchamel sauce

30 g unsalted butter

30 g plain flour

400 ml milk

salt and freshly ground black pepper

1 Preheat the oven to Gas Mark 4/180°C. Bake the potatoes for 1 hour or until soft when pierced.

2 Remove the potatoes from the oven, cut in half and press through a drum sieve (see page 9), discarding the skin. Place in a bowl. Pour the milk and butter into a pan and bring to a simmer. Mix in to the potato slowly, using a spatula. Season.

3 Make the béchamel sauce. Melt the butter in a pan and slowly add the flour. Cook for 5 minutes, stirring with a spoon. Gradually pour in the milk a little at a time, stirring continuously until you obtain a smooth velvety sauce. Season to taste.

4 Place the fish and peas into an ovenproof dish around 20 x 20 cm. Season and add a squeeze of lemon juice. Pour over the béchamel sauce. Spoon on the mash, starting at the edges and working towards the centre. Bake in the oven for 40 minutes. Serve with a green salad.

make it sensational

'sensational'

Elegant fish pies

Making individual portions of home comfort dishes such as fish or shepherd's pie is a fantastic way of making it more refined. The mussels and prawns make the presentation rather dramatic.

Serves 4

1 Mash recipe (previous page)

400 g mixed salmon, cod and smoked
    haddock, cut into chunks

100 g frozen peas

salt and freshly ground black pepper

8 large fresh mussels

8 king prawns, peeled and tails left on

For the fish sauce

20 g unsalted butter

2 shallots, finely chopped

6 button mushrooms, sliced

100 ml white wine

400 ml fish stock (see Tip on
    page 26)

100 ml double cream

salt and freshly ground black pepper

juice of ½ lemon

1 Preheat the oven to Gas Mark 4/180°C. Make the Mash.

2 For the fish sauce, melt the butter in a pan. Add the shallots and cook for 3–4 minutes, then add the mushrooms and cook for a further 2 minutes. Pour in the white wine and reduce until almost dry. Add the fish stock, bring to the boil and reduce by half, then pour in the double cream, bring to the boil again and take off the heat. Season to taste, add a squeeze of lemon juice and strain through a sieve.

3 Divide the fish and peas between four ramekins 7 cm in diameter and 6 cm high. Season and pour in the fish sauce to just cover the fish. Spoon the mash into a piping bag and top each ramekin with the mash, swirling to make a pattern. If you don't have a piping bag, use a fork to make a pattern. Insert two mussels (narrow end down) and two king prawns (tail sticking out) into each portion of mash.

4 Bake in the oven for 15 minutes or until the mash is golden brown and the mussels have opened.

Transform this pie from homely to elegant by making it in individual dishes and garnishing with shellfish in step 3

see pictures overleaf

'simple'

'Present each person with their own mini fish pie.'

'sensational'

'simple'

Roast cod with creamy cabbage, Parma ham, carrot and celeriac

Nowadays, you can buy farmed cod that is more sustainable than the wild variety. If you can't find it, use pollock instead.

Serves 4

4 x 150 g pieces of cod, skin removed

salt and freshly ground black pepper

a drizzle of olive oil

20 g unsalted butter

juice of ½ lemon

For the creamy cabbage

½ Savoy cabbage, finely chopped

salt

iced water

50 ml olive oil

2 carrots, peeled and cut into
   1 cm cubes

¼ celeriac, peeled and cut into
   1 cm cubes

1 garlic clove, crushed

1 teaspoon caraway seeds

25 g unsalted butter

4 slices Parma ham, shredded

freshly ground black pepper

2 tablespoons crème fraîche

1 Preheat the oven to Gas Mark 4/180°C.

2 Cook the cabbage in boiling salted water for 3 minutes, then remove with a slotted spoon and plunge into iced water. Drain and squeeze out the excess water.

3 Heat the olive oil in a pan and add the carrots and celeriac. Cook for 6 minutes, then add the garlic, caraway seeds, butter and Parma ham. Cook for 2 minutes. Test that the carrot and celeriac are cooked, then add the cabbage. Warm through, season, add the crème fraîche and cook for a further 1 minute.

4 Season the cod pieces, heat the olive oil in a frying pan and cook the fish for 3 minutes until golden brown. Flip over, add the butter and place in the oven for 5 minutes. Take out and add a squeeze of lemon juice.

5 To serve, spoon the cabbage on to a plate and place a piece of cod on top.

'sensational'

Cod wrapped in Parma ham with cabbage pesto

Cod works especially well with meats such as chorizo and bacon. For this recipe to work you need to use pieces of cod from a large fish rather than small fillets. The cabbage pesto is delicious tossed with warm pasta.

Serves 4

**1 Creamy Cabbage recipe
(previous page), but without the
Parma ham**

4 x 150 g cod pieces

salt and freshly ground black pepper

4 slices Parma ham

a drizzle of olive oil

20 g unsalted butter

For the cabbage pesto

20 g pine nuts

**outer green leaves of 1 Savoy
cabbage**

salt

iced water

30 g freshly grated Parmesan

½ garlic clove

200 ml extra virgin olive oil

freshly ground black pepper

1 Make the Creamy Cabbage, but without the Parma ham.

2 To make the pesto, put the pine nuts in a dry frying pan and heat gently until toasted and golden brown all over. Set to one side.

3 Cook the cabbage leaves in boiling salted water for 5 minutes or until soft, remove with a slotted spoon and plunge into iced water. Drain and squeeze out the excess water. Place in a blender with all the other cabbage pesto ingredients, including the toasted pine nuts, whizz and season to taste.

4 Lightly season the cod and wrap one slice of Parma ham around each piece of fish. Wrap tightly in cling film. Bring a pan of water to the boil and use a steamer to steam the cod for 5 minutes to hold the shape and secure the Parma ham

5 Heat a little olive oil in a pan and fry the cod pieces for 2 minutes on one side. Flip over, add the butter and cook for another 2 minutes (test with a cocktail stick to make sure the fish is done; see Tip on page 80).

6 To serve, spoon the cabbage pesto on to a plate, slightly to one side, add the creamy cabbage and top with the cod.

sensational

'The quality of the meat will determine the quality of the dish, so always buy the best you can afford.'

Jun

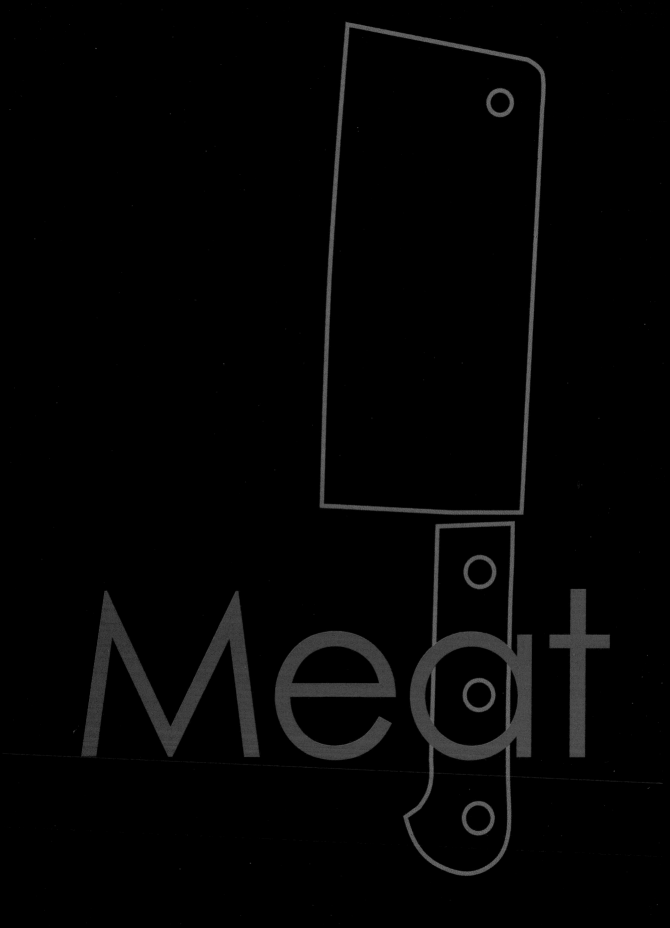

'simple'

Quick fried lamb steak with crushed peas and broad beans and mint dressing

Lamb steaks are a fantastic alternative for barbecues. Try marinating them the day before in 4 tablespoons of natural Greek yoghurt, a crushed garlic clove, the juice from 1 lime, 1 tablespoon of honey and chopped fresh rosemary. The mint sauce will keep in the fridge for a week.

Serves 4

4 x 250 g lamb steaks

a drizzle of olive oil

For the crushed peas and broad beans

120 g broad beans

salt

120 g peas (fresh or frozen)

1 garlic clove, crushed

1 tablespoon crème fraîche

freshly ground black pepper

For the mint sauce

1 bunch fresh mint leaves

2 tablespoons caster sugar

30 ml white wine vinegar

a pinch of salt

50 ml extra virgin olive oil

1 To make the mint sauce, pick the mint leaves and place in a pestle and mortar. Add the sugar and grind into a paste. Add the vinegar, a pinch of salt and the olive oil. Mix together well.

2 Cook the broad beans in boiling salted water for 2 minutes, then remove with a slotted spoon and plunge into iced water. Drain, remove the outer skin of the broad beans and discard. Keep the broad beans to one side.

3 Cook the peas for 2 minutes and then place in the iced water. Drain and add to the broad beans. Roughly crush the peas and broad beans using a fork and add the garlic, crème fraîche and seasoning.

4 Season the lamb on both sides and lightly drizzle with olive oil. Cook on a hot griddle for 3 minutes on each side.

5 To serve, place the crushed peas and broad beans in a pan and gently warm through. Spoon the peas and beans on to a plate, place a lamb steak on top and drizzle with the mint sauce.

SIMPLE

'sensational'

Herb crushed lamb with peas, broad beans and smoked bacon

This is spring on a plate. The loin of lamb from the best end is quite expensive, so for a cheaper option try using the neck fillet.

Serves 4

1 Mint Sauce recipe (previous page)
1 Crushed Peas and Broad Beans
    recipe (previous page)
100 g streaky smoked bacon, cut into
    small pieces
2 tablespoons olive oil
2 medium free range egg whites
4 x 150 g loin lamb (the meat from
    the best end, with no bones or fat)
salt and freshly ground black pepper
25 g butter
1 tablespoon crème fraîche

For the herb crust

2 slices white bread
a sprig of fresh thyme
a sprig of fresh rosemary
1 bunch fresh parsley
1 garlic clove
salt and freshly ground black pepper

1   Make the Mint Sauce.

2   Make the Crushed Peas and Broad Beans. Fry the smoked bacon in 1 tablespoon of olive oil until crisp and add to the peas and broad beans.

3   Preheat the oven to Gas Mark ¼/110ºC. Make the herb crust. Place the bread on a baking tray and dry in the oven for 2 hours until crisp. Break up and place in a blender with the leaves from the thyme, rosemary and parsley. Add the garlic and whizz until you obtain green breadcrumbs. Season and place the herb crumbs on a plate.

4   Increase the oven temperature to Gas Mark 6/ 200ºC.

5   Pour the egg whites on to a plate and whisk with a fork. Season the lamb, dip in the egg white, then dip in the herb crumbs and coat well, pressing the crumbs on to the meat.

6   To cook the lamb, heat the remaining olive oil and the butter in a frying pan. Once the butter has melted, add the lamb and cook for 30 seconds. Flip over and place in the oven for 5 minutes. Remove and leave to rest for 3–4 minutes.

7   To serve, warm the peas and broad beans in a pan and spoon on to a plate. Cut the lamb into slices and place on top of the peas and broad beans. Finally, put a drizzle of mint sauce and a little crème fraîche on the side.

see picture overleaf

Lamb, fresh green peas
and broad beans make
this taste like spring
on a plate.

'sensational'

'simple'

Simple lamb casserole with onions and new potatoes

Casseroles always taste better the day after they're cooked. It gives the ingredients time to fully release their flavours and combine them. However, if you don't have time, this casserole is still delicious eaten on the day.

Serves 4
50 ml vegetable oil
800 g lamb neck fillets, cut into
　　4 cm pieces
salt and freshly ground black pepper
12 button onions, peeled
4 medium carrots, peeled and
　　thickly sliced
1 tablespoon tomato purée
300 ml white wine
300 ml Madeira
12 new potatoes, peeled and
　　left whole
4 whole garlic cloves
3 plum tomatoes, roughly chopped
a sprig of fresh thyme
a sprig of fresh rosemary
800 ml lamb stock (see Tip on
　　page 26)
½ bunch fresh mint, leaves chopped,
　　to serve

1　Preheat the oven to Gas Mark 4/180°C.

2　Heat half the vegetable oil in a frying pan. Season the lamb pieces and fry for 5 minutes until caramelised all over.

3　While the lamb is cooking, heat the remaining oil in a separate ovenproof casserole dish. Fry the button onions and carrots for 3–4 minutes until browned. Add the tomato purée and cook for a further 2 minutes.

4　Drain the lamb in a colander. Pour the white wine and Madeira into the frying pan, bring to the boil and scrape off the sediment from the bottom of the pan. Add to the vegetables in the casserole dish.

5　Add the lamb, potatoes, garlic, tomatoes, thyme, rosemary and stock to the casserole. The liquid should just cover the meat (add extra stock if it doesn't). Bring to the boil and place a circular piece of baking parchment over the lamb and vegetables. Cover with a lid and cook for 1½–2 hours or until the lamb is tender. Remove the herb sprigs and season to taste.

6　To serve, spoon into large bowls and scatter over the chopped mint leaves.

Tip
When choosing cuts of meat for a casserole, buy something with a little fat, as this will prevent the meat from becoming too dry.

'sensational'

Rich lamb casserole with baby vegetables

Casseroles are normally associated with autumn and winter, but this is a spring dish – my version of the French 'Navarin d'agneau'. It features regularly on my lunch menu in the restaurant.

Serves 4

1 Simple Lamb Casserole with Onions and New Potatoes recipe (previous page), but without the new potatoes
12 new potatoes, peeled
salt
iced water
120 g peas (fresh or frozen)
12 baby leeks
12 baby carrots, scraped clean
35 g unsalted butter

Tip
Reducing the cooking liquid with the cooked pieces of meat adds moisture and intensifies their flavour. You can do this with all braised meats and you'll see what a difference it'll make.

1 Make the Simple Lamb Casserole with Onions and New Potatoes, but do not add the potatoes.

2 While the casserole is in the oven, place the new potatoes in a pan, cover with cold water, season with salt and cook for 10–15 minutes until soft.

3 Bring a pan of salted water to the boil and cook the peas for 2 minutes. Remove with a slotted spoon and plunge into iced water. Cook the leeks for 3–4 minutes, then remove to iced water. Cook the carrots for 5 minutes, then place in the iced water. When cold, drain the vegetables.

4 Once the casserole is cooked, remove from the oven and leave to cool for 1 hour. Carefully transfer the lamb to a large ovenproof frying pan, making sure the pieces are not on top of each other. Preheat the oven to Gas Mark 6/200°C.

5 Strain the casserole liquid through a fine sieve over a saucepan. Discard the vegetables. Ladle some of the liquid over the meat, bring to a boil and place in the oven for 10–15 minutes. Occasionally open the oven to spoon the juices over the meat. As the liquid reduces it will become rich and sticky, coating the pieces of lamb.

6 Heat the remaining liquid in a pan and reduce by a third. Place the potatoes and vegetables into a pan, add 100 ml of hot water, the butter and seasoning and warm through.

7 Once the lamb is shiny and glazed, remove from the oven. Place four or five pieces in a bowl, spoon over some of the vegetables, pour over the sauce and finish with scattered mint leaves.

see pictures overleaf

sensational

'simple'

'Reducing the liquid at the end of
the cooking really intensifies flavour.'

'sensational'

'simple'

Chargrilled pork chop with sweet and sour peppers

Pork naturally marries well with sweet, tart flavours. Don't make the common mistake of over-cooking the pork, as this will make it dry and tough.

SIMPLE

Serves 4
4 pork chops, French trimmed
salt and freshly ground black pepper
a drizzle of olive oil
For the sweet and sour peppers
100 ml olive oil
1 yellow pepper, de-seeded and
   sliced
1 red pepper, de-seeded and sliced
½ red chilli, de-seeded and sliced
salt and freshly ground black pepper
¼ pineapple, peeled and cut into 2 cm
   chunks
2 tablespoons caster sugar
50 ml white wine vinegar

make it sensational

1 Make the sweet and sour peppers. Heat half the olive oil in a pan and fry the peppers and chilli for 4 minutes. Season and add the pineapple. Cook for a further 2 minutes, add the sugar and vinegar, stir well and cook for a final minute. Keep warm.

2 Preheat the oven to Gas Mark 6/200°C.

3 Season the pork chops, drizzle with olive oil on both sides and cook on a hot griddle for 2 minutes on each side. Transfer to a baking tray and finish in the oven for 8 minutes.

4 To serve, spoon the sweet and sour peppers on to a plate and top with a pork chop.

✳ French trimming gives a cleaner, more refined appearance. You can do it yourself by trimming down to the bone or ask your butcher to do it for you.

'sensational'

Glazed pork chop with peppers and herb dressing

The glaze for this pork is a versatile marinade that works with chicken, rabbit or beef. Smear it over the meat 5 minutes before it finishes cooking. The herb dressing is delicious with seafood.

Serves 4

Chargrilled Pork Chop with Sweet and Sour Peppers recipe (previous page)

For the herb dressing

¼ bunch fresh flat leaf parsley, finely chopped
¼ bunch fresh basil, finely chopped
¼ bunch fresh mint, finely chopped
1 tablespoon Dijon mustard
1 tablespoon capers, chopped
1 garlic clove, crushed
juice of ½ lemon
100 ml extra virgin olive oil
salt and freshly ground black pepper

For the glaze

2 tablespoons tomato purée
1 tablespoon red wine vinegar
1 tablespoon soy sauce
1 tablespoon honey

1 To make the herb dressing, combine all the ingredients in a bowl and season to taste.

2 For the glaze, mix the ingredients together in a bowl.

3 Cook the sweet and sour peppers.

4 Preheat the oven to Gas Mark 6/200°C.

5 Griddle the pork chops. Smear both sides with the glaze before cooking them in the oven. Cook for 8 minutes.

6 To serve, spoon the peppers on to a plate, trim the bottom of the pork with a knife so it sits upright and drizzle the herb dressing on top.

sensational

Spoon a tangy glaze on to the pork chop (see step 5)

see pictures overleaf

'simple'

'A honey glaze and a herb dressing
transform this simple pork chop.'

'sensational'

'simple'

Spiced venison with stir-fried red cabbage and honey roast butternut squash

Venison is one of the healthiest red meats available and is always free range. It's normally eaten during the game season in autumn, but you can buy good quality farmed venison all year round. It works really well with spices and fruits and is no more difficult to cook than any other meat.

Serves 4

1 Granny Smith apple, cored but not peeled

2 carrots, peeled and halved

50 ml olive oil, plus an extra 3 tablespoons

¼ red cabbage, finely shredded

1 red onion, finely sliced

salt and freshly ground black pepper

75 ml red wine vinegar

½ butternut squash, peeled, de-seeded and cut into small chunks

50 g unsalted butter

1 tablespoon runny honey

4 x 150 g venison loins with no sinew

For the spice mix

30 g juniper berries

30 g whole black peppercorns

Tip

When you plan a stir fry, cut all the ingredients into small even pieces so they cook quickly and at the same rate.

1 To make the spice mix, lightly fry the spices in a dry frying pan for 3–4 minutes. Blend in a food processor until very finely ground. The spices will keep in a airtight plastic container for weeks.

2 Slice the apple on a Japanese mandolin (see page 9) and cut into matchstick-sized pieces. Cut the carrots in half, slice on the mandolin and cut into matchsticks. Heat 50 ml of olive oil in a frying pan, add the cabbage, carrots and red onion and fry for 4 minutes. Add the apple, cook for a further 1 minute, season and add the vinegar. Keep warm.

3 Heat 2 tablespoons of olive oil in a pan, add the squash and fry for 3–4 minutes until golden brown. Season, add half the butter and cook for a further 5 minutes or until the butternut squash is soft. Finally add the honey and coat the squash.

4 Preheat the oven to Gas Mark 6/200°C.

5 To cook the venison, season with salt, pour the spices on to a plate and roll the venison in the spices. Heat a drizzle of olive oil in an ovenproof pan, add the venison and cook for 1 minute. Flip over, add the remaining butter and place in the oven for 6–8 minutes. Take out and leave to rest for 4 minutes.

6 To serve, spoon the cabbage on to a plate, scatter the butternut squash around, slice the venison into four and place on top of the red cabbage.

'sensational'

Spiced venison with braised red cabbage and butternut squash purée

Venison and red cabbage is a popular combination because the sweet taste of the cabbage works so well with the spiced venison.

Serves 4

1 Spice Mix recipe (previous page)
4 x 150 g venison loins with no sinew
salt
a drizzle of olive oil
25 g unsalted butter

For the braised red cabbage
50 ml olive oil
2 red onions, halved and finely sliced
2 garlic cloves, sliced
½ red cabbage, finely shredded
salt and freshly ground black pepper
50 ml red wine vinegar
125 ml red wine
125 ml cassis (blackcurrant liqueur)
1 cinnamon stick
a sprig of fresh thyme
2 pieces orange peel
1 tablespoon redcurrant jelly

For the butternut squash purée
50 g unsalted butter
300 g peeled, de-seeded and diced
    butternut squash
100 ml chicken stock (see Tip on
    page 26)
50 ml double cream
salt and freshly ground black pepper

1 Make the Spice Mix. Preheat the oven to Gas Mark 4/180°C.

2 For the cabbage, heat the oil in an ovenproof dish, add the red onions and garlic, cover and cook on a gentle heat for 5 minutes. Turn up the heat, add the cabbage and season. Cook for 2 minutes. Add the vinegar, red wine, cassis, cinnamon, thyme and orange peel. Bring to the boil, cover with a disc of baking parchment, put a lid on top and bake in the oven for 2 hours until the cabbage is soft. Take out of the oven and stir in the redcurrant jelly. Correct the seasoning.

3 For the butternut squash purée, melt the butter in a pan and fry the squash very gently with a lid on for 5 minutes. Add the stock, bring to the boil, reduce the heat and simmer for 10 minutes until soft. Add the double cream, bring to the boil, then remove from the heat and whizz in a blender until smooth. Season to taste.

4 Increase the oven temperature to Gas Mark 6/200°C.

5 To cook the venison, season with salt, pour the spices on to a plate and roll the venison in the spices. Heat a drizzle of olive oil in an ovenproof pan, add the venison and cook for 1 minute. Flip over, add the butter and place in the oven for 6–8 minutes. Take out and leave to rest for 4 minutes.

6 To serve, spoon the cabbage on to a plate, slice the venison and carefully arrange on top. Finish with a spoon of purée to the side.

'simple'

Griddled chicken with chorizo and butter bean mash

Butter beans make a quick and easy alternative to mashed potatoes. You can use any kind of tinned beans. This is so easy you can cook this dish in less time than it takes to microwave a meal.

SIMPLE

Serves 4

4 boneless, skinless free range
    chicken breasts
salt and freshly ground black pepper
50 ml olive oil
For the butter bean mash
410 g can butter beans, drained and
    rinsed
1 garlic clove
100 ml olive oil
salt and freshly ground black pepper
For the chorizo and peppers
50 ml olive oil
200 g chorizo, sliced
1 red pepper, de-seeded and sliced
1 yellow pepper, de-seeded and
    sliced
1 red onion, sliced
salt and freshly ground black pepper
1 garlic clove, crushed
½ red chilli, finely chopped
1 tablespoon sherry vinegar
½ bunch fresh basil, roughly
    shredded

1 Carefully cut the chicken horizontally almost all the way through the middle and open out. Season. Drizzle with the olive oil and place on a hot griddle for 4–5 minutes. Flip over and cook for a further 3 minutes until the chicken is cooked through.

2 To make the butter bean mash, pour the beans into a saucepan with the garlic and 100 ml water. Bring to the boil and cook for 2–3 minutes, stirring occasionally. Remove from the heat and whizz in a blender with the olive oil until smooth. Season to taste.

3 Pour the remaining oil into a pan, add the chorizo, peppers and onion and cook for 5 minutes. Season, add the garlic and chilli, cook for another 1 minute and finally add the sherry vinegar and shredded basil.

4 To serve, spoon the butter bean mash on to a plate, top with the chicken, then the chorizo and peppers.

Tip
Cutting meat horizontally almost all the way through the middle and opening it out is called 'butterflying'. When prepared in this way, it cooks in half the time.

sensational

Roast chicken stuffed with sun-dried tomato butter, white beans and chorizo

I don't think it's possible to cook a perfect roast chicken when it's whole. The breasts will always cook quicker than the legs. When I cook chicken at home I always remove the legs and cook them separately or use them in a casserole or curry.

Serves 4

2 free range chicken crowns (the whole chicken without the legs)
50 ml olive oil
salt and freshly ground black pepper
1 Chorizo and Peppers recipe (previous page)
410 g can butter beans, dried and rinsed

For the sun-dried tomato butter

10 sun-dried tomatoes in olive oil
1 garlic clove
40 g dried breadcrumbs
2 tablespoons freshly grated Parmesan
75 g unsalted butter, softened

1 Preheat the oven to Gas Mark 6/200°C.

2 Make the sun-dried tomato butter by blending the tomatoes and garlic to form a smooth paste. Put the tomato paste in a bowl and stir in the breadcrumbs, Parmesan and butter.

3 Stuff the chicken crowns. Using your fingers, lift the skin off the breast very gently from the neck end, pushing down towards the base to make a pocket and leaving the sides intact. Put the tomato butter into a piping bag (see page 9) and pipe under the skin all over the breasts. Spread very gently with your fingers, making sure that the skin doesn't break. Brush the chicken lightly with olive oil, season, place on a baking tray and roast in the oven for 20 minutes. Once the chicken is cooked, remove from the oven, cover with aluminium foil and rest for 10 minutes.

4 While the chicken is resting, make the Chorizo and Peppers. Add the beans at the end and warm through.

5 To serve, remove the chicken breasts using a sharp knife and serve on top of the chorizo, peppers and beans.

Tip
Stuffing the chicken with the tomato butter will keep the breasts really moist so there's no need to baste it while cooking.

'simple'

Duck breast with caramelised chicory and lentils

Duck is easy to cook. You don't need to use any extra oil because there's enough fat on the breasts. The orange juice cuts through the richness and the lentils add earthiness.

SIMPLE

Serves 4

4 duck breasts

For the lentils

200 g Puy lentils

1 carrot, peeled and cut in half

1 onion, cut in half

1 rasher streaky bacon

a sprig of fresh thyme

1 garlic clove

½ chicken stock cube

50 ml olive oil

2 tablespoons sherry vinegar

salt and freshly ground black pepper

For the caramelised chicory

40 g unsalted butter

**2 chicory, cut into quarters
    lengthways**

salt and freshly ground black pepper

20 g caster sugar

30 g fresh ginger, peeled and sliced

juice of 4 oranges

Tip

Unlike other dried beans you don't need to soak lentils before cooking. Just boil them once and then go ahead and cook them.

1 Put the lentils in a pan, cover with cold water and bring to the boil. Drain and cover with fresh cold water. Add the carrot, onion, bacon, thyme, garlic and chicken stock cube. Cook on a gentle simmer for 30 minutes or until the lentils are tender (do not overcook). Once cooked, leave to cool in the liquid.

2 For the chicory, melt the butter in a frying pan and arrange the chicory in a single layer. Season and fry for 2 minutes. Turn the chicory over using a spatula, sprinkle over the sugar, add the ginger and cook for 2 minutes. Pour in the orange juice and cook for a further 6–8 minutes (the chicory should still be slightly crunchy).

3 Preheat the oven to Gas Mark 6/200°C.

4 Season the duck breasts and place skin side down in a cold, dry, ovenproof frying pan (there is no need to add butter or oil as there is enough fat on the duck breasts). Heat the frying pan (this helps to render the fat, resulting in a crispy skin). Cook skin side down for 6–8 minutes or until caramelised. Flip the duck breasts over and place in the oven for 5 minutes. Remove from the oven and leave to rest for 5 minutes.

5 Drain the lentils, pick out the onion, carrot, bacon, thyme and garlic. Place the lentils in a bowl and pour in the olive oil and vinegar. Place back in the pan, season and gently warm through.

6 To serve, spoon the lentils on to a plate, place the duck breast to the side and arrange the chicory.

see picture overleaf

'sensational'

Home smoked duck breast with chicory and lentil salsa

Smoking food at home is a lot easier than it sounds. All you need is a metal steamer (see page 9) lined with aluminium foil. Once you've got the hang of it, try smoking fresh mackerel or salmon – delicious!

Serves 4

4 duck breasts

20 g fresh tea leaves (Lapsang Souchong or Darjeeling)

salt and freshly ground black pepper

1 Caramelised Chicory recipe (previous page)

For the lentil salsa

1 Lentil recipe (previous page)

25 ml olive oil

4 rashers streaky bacon, finely chopped

1 red pepper, de-seeded and finely chopped

1 green pepper, de-seeded and finely chopped

½ red chilli, de-seeded and finely chopped

1 tablespoon sherry vinegar

½ bunch spring onions, finely chopped

1 tablespoon chopped fresh coriander

salt and freshly ground black pepper

1 Preheat the oven to Gas Mark 6/200°C.

2 To smoke the duck breasts, line the bottom of a stainless steel steamer with aluminium foil, pour in the fresh tea, place the top half and lid back on and place on the heat. Wait for 5 minutes or until the tea starts to smoke, then place the duck breasts skin side up in the steamer. Cover with the lid and smoke for 6 minutes.

3 Remove the duck, season, place skin side up in a cold, dry, ovenproof frying pan and heat. Cook for 6–8 minutes until caramelised, then flip over and place in the oven for 5 minutes. Take out and leave to rest for 5 minutes.

4 Make the Lentils.

5 Heat the olive oil in a frying pan, add the bacon and fry for 3–4 minutes until golden brown. Add the peppers and chilli, cook for 2 minutes then add the vinegar. Mix the peppers and bacon with the cooked lentils, add the spring onions, fresh coriander and seasoning and mix.

6 Make the Caramelised Chicory.

7 To serve, spoon the lentils into a bowl, slice the duck breasts and arrange on top and finish with the chicory.

'simple'

Duck is really easy to cook. This quick dish is earthy and satisfying.

'simple'

Steak and chips with Béarnaise sauce

You can't get more classic than steak, chips and Béarnaise sauce, but I still don't get tired of it. This is as simple as it gets. Béarnaise is one of my favourite sauces and works well with lamb, chicken, salmon, sea bass and, actually, pretty much anything!

Serves 4

4 x 200 g sirloin steaks

salt and freshly ground black pepper

1 tablespoon vegetable oil

25 g unsalted butter

For the Béarnaise sauce

1 shallot, finely chopped

1 teaspoon black peppercorns

200 ml white wine vinegar

4 medium free range egg yolks

a pinch of salt

250 g unsalted butter, melted and hot

a sprig of fresh tarragon, chopped

For the chips

1 kg potatoes (Désirée, Maris Piper or
    King Edward), peeled and cut into
    2 cm thick chips

salt

50 ml vegetable oil

freshly ground black pepper

1 To make the Béarnaise sauce, place the shallot, peppercorns and vinegar in a small pan, bring to the boil and reduce by half. Pour through a sieve and discard the shallots and black peppercorns. Place the egg yolks in a blender with a pinch of salt and 2 tablespoons of the reduced vinegar. Start to blend and very slowly pour in the hot, melted butter. If the sauce starts to get too thick, add a tablespoon of warm water. Check the seasoning, add a touch more vinegar if necessary and stir in the chopped tarragon.

2 Place a roasting tray in the oven and preheat to Gas Mark 7/220°C.

3 Par-boil the potatoes in a pan of salted water for about 6–8 minutes or until just tender when pierced with a skewer. Very carefully drain and dry with kitchen paper. Remove the preheated roasting tray, add the vegetable oil, then the potatoes, season and place back in the oven. Cook for 15–20 minutes, turning the chips occasionally. When crisp and golden take out of the oven and drain on kitchen paper.

4 Season the steaks. Add the oil to a hot frying pan and cook the steaks for 3–5 minutes on each side, adding the butter for the last 2 minutes of cooking. For medium rare, the steaks should be slightly springy when pressed. Take out and rest for 5 minutes.

5 To serve, place a steak on a plate with chips and a generous dollop of Béarnaise sauce.

'sensational'

Beef fillet cooked in a thyme-infused salt crust, chips and Béarnaise sauce

This is the best way to cook beef fillet. The salt and thyme penetrate the meat, giving it a wonderful aroma and flavour. Crack it open in front of your guests for a dramatic effect.

Serves 4

1 Chips recipe (previous page)
1 Béarnaise Sauce recipe
   (previous page)
2 tablespoons vegetable oil
800 g beef fillet
freshly ground black pepper
For the thyme-infused salt crust
3 bunches fresh thyme, chopped
500 g coarse sea salt
1 medium free range egg
400 g strong white bread or pasta
   flour, plus extra for dusting

1 Make the salt crust. In a large bowl combine the thyme, salt, egg and 100 ml water. Mix well and gradually add the flour, until a firm, elastic dough is formed. If it's too dry, add a touch more water. If it's too wet, add a little more flour. Cover with cling film and leave at room temperature for 1 hour.

2 Make the Chips and Béarnaise Sauce.

3 Once the salt crust has rested, preheat the oven to Gas Mark 7/220°C. Roll out the dough on a lightly floured surface to form a circle roughly 30 cm in diameter and around 0.5 cm thick.

4 Heat the oil in a frying pan, season the beef with pepper and fry for 2–3 minutes, turning regularly until browned on all sides.

5 Place the beef in the centre of the dough circle and cut through the dough at right angles from each corner of the fillet. Remove the excess squares of dough to leave the beef in the centre of a wide cross shape. Bring the dough up and over the beef to fully enclose, pressing firmly with your fingers to seal. Patch up any holes using the leftover dough. Turn over and place on a baking tray. Make a hole in the top with a skewer. Bake in the oven for 18–20 minutes for rare. Once cooked, remove from the oven and leave to rest in the crust for 15 minutes.

6 To serve, break open the crust with your hands and discard. Pat the beef with kitchen paper to remove excess salt. Cut into four equal portions and serve with the chips and Béarnaise sauce.

Tip
To check how well the beef is cooked, insert a metal skewer into the hole at the top so it's halfway through the beef. Leave for 10 seconds, pull out and carefully touch it. It should feel warm.

sensational

'Always use vegetables that are in season, they will be bursting with flavour and reasonably priced.'

Jun

Vegetables

'simple'

Asparagus hollandaise

This is the classic way to eat asparagus. Making hollandaise sauce can seem like a daunting task but this is an easy method. The secret is to add the melted butter very slowly. Hollandaise is such a versatile sauce that once you've mastered it, you'll be eating it with everything!

Serves 4

20 asparagus spears

250 g butter

3 medium free range egg yolks

juice of ½ lemon, plus extra if needed

salt and freshly ground black pepper

1 Trim away the hard root of the asparagus about 2 cm from the bottom. Peel using a potato peeler by holding the tip with one hand and running the peeler along the stem.

2 Put the butter into a pan and bring to the boil, then remove from the heat. Place the eggs in a blender, squeeze in the lemon juice and start to blend gently. Very, very slowly pour the melted butter on to the eggs. The eggs and butter will slowly emulsify and thicken like mayonnaise. If it gets too thick, add a drop of hot water. Season and add more lemon juice if needed.

3 Bring a large pot of water to the boil, season with salt and add the asparagus. Cook for around 3–4 minutes. Drain.

4 To serve, place five spears on each plate with a large dollop of hollandaise.

Tip

Adding salt to the water when boiling green vegetables not only seasons them but also helps to retain their colour. If you're not serving the vegetables immediately after cooking, plunge into iced water. This also helps to retain their vibrant colour. When serving, re-warm in hot water for 1 minute.

SIMPLE

Grilled asparagus, crisp poached egg and Parmesan

Deep-fried poached eggs are impressive and so simple. They also work beautifully with smoked haddock or in a warm salad with leeks and mushrooms.

Serves 4

100 ml white wine vinegar
4 medium free range eggs
iced water
25 g plain flour
1 medium free range egg, beaten
50 g Panko (Japanese breadcrumbs)
   or normal breadcrumbs
salt and freshly ground black pepper
12 asparagus spears
1 tablespoon olive oil
sunflower or groundnut oil, for frying
2 tablespoons freshly grated
   Parmesan

1 Fill a tall pan with water, add vinegar to 'cook' the eggs more quickly and place on the heat.

2 Wait until you can see streams of small bubbles rising to the surface – this is just before the water starts to boil. Break an egg into a cup, then quickly pour into the water when you see the small bubbles. Repeat with each egg. As the bubbles rise to the surface, they will help to push the white of the egg up and around the yolk.

3 Poach the eggs for 3 minutes, then carefully lift out with a spoon and add to iced water.

4 To coat the eggs, carefully dry with a cloth. Place the flour, beaten egg and breadcrumbs on separate dishes. Season the poached eggs, coat in the flour, then in the egg and finally in the breadcrumbs. Keep to one side.

5 Trim away the hard root of the asparagus about 2 cm off the bottom. Peel using a potato peeler by holding the tip with one hand and running the peeler along the stem. Lightly coat the asparagus in olive oil, season and place on a hot griddle for 3 minutes, turning occasionally.

6 Half fill a pan with oil and heat until a pinch of breadcrumbs sizzles when dropped into the oil. If you have a deep fat fryer, heat it to 180°C. Deep fry the eggs for 30 seconds.

7 To serve, place three asparagus spears on each plate, sprinkle with Parmesan and top with an egg.

'simple'

Creamy garlic potatoes

Recipes don't get more simple than this. This makes a fantastic accompaniment for any Sunday roast. It's my favourite potato dish and is one of the first recipes I learnt how to make at Le Gavroche. I'm still not tired of it!

Serves 4
125 ml full-fat milk
200 ml double cream
1 garlic clove, crushed
a sprig of fresh rosemary
salt and freshly ground black pepper
2 large Désirée potatoes

1 Preheat the oven to Gas Mark 4/180°C.

2 Pour the milk and cream into a pan, add the garlic and rosemary, season well and bring to a simmer. Take off the heat and keep to one side.

3 Peel the potatoes and slice on a mandolin (see page 9) to get slices 3 mm in thickness. Place in a large bowl. Pour the milk and cream over the potatoes and pick out the sprig of rosemary. Mix well so each slice of potato is coated in liquid.

4 Lay a single layer of potato on the bottom of an ovenproof dish 20 x 10 cm and 5 cm high. Spoon over 2–3 tablespoons of the cream and repeat the process until all the potatoes are used up.

5 Bake in the oven for 45 minutes. To check whether it is cooked, pierce the gratin with a small knife. If it slides in easily it's ready. If the top of the gratin turns golden before it's ready, cover with aluminium foil and finish cooking.

Tip
There are literally hundreds of different varieties of potato, but they can basically be divided into either waxy or floury. Cooking fantastic potato dishes is all about choosing the right variety for the recipe. As a basic rule, for roast potatoes and chips use floury potatoes like King Edwards, Maris Piper or Golden Wonder. For gratins or simply boiled for salads, choose the waxy varieties like Jersey Royals, Charlottes or Désirée.

SIMPLE

'sensational'

Celeriac, potato and truffle gratin

This gratin is good enough to turn people vegetarian. It's so tasty and refined it should be eaten as the centrepiece of a dish rather than as an accompaniment. Serve a simple green salad as a garnish. If you can't get hold of fresh truffle, add a teaspoon of truffle oil to the milk and cream.

Serves 4

125 ml full-fat milk
200 ml double cream
1 garlic clove, crushed
a sprig of fresh rosemary
salt and freshly ground black pepper
1 large Désirée potato
½ celeriac
6 slices truffle
a handful freshly grated Gruyère or
    Parmesan

* By simply adding the celeriac and truffle, the dish has been given a new dimension of flavour.

1 Preheat the oven to Gas Mark 4/180°C.

2 Pour the milk and cream into a pan, add the garlic and rosemary, season well and bring to a simmer. Take off the heat and keep to one side.

3 Peel the potato and celeriac and slice on a mandolin (see page 9) to get slices 3 mm in thickness. Place them in separate bowls. Pour half the cream and milk over the potatoes and the other half over the celeriac. Mix well.

4 Lay a single layer of potato on the bottom of an ovenproof dish 20 x 10 cm and 5 cm high. Spoon over 2–3 tablespoons of the liquid. Alternate the layers of potato and celeriac, adding a layer of sliced truffles halfway through. Once all of the slices are used, place in the oven for 45 minutes. About 10 minutes before the gratin has finished cooking, sprinkle over the cheese. Finish off in the oven.

'simple'

Wild mushrooms and caramelised onions on brioche

This is my version of mushrooms on toast – a classic!

Serves 4

50 ml olive oil

2 large onions, cut in half and finely sliced

1 garlic clove, crushed

salt and freshly ground black pepper

40 ml white wine vinegar

1 tablespoon caster sugar

20 g unsalted butter

300 g mixed wild mushrooms, washed

a sprig of fresh thyme, leaves stripped and chopped

juice of ½ lemon

4 x 2 cm thick slices brioche

a handful of Parmesan shavings

1 Heat the olive oil in a pan and add the onions and garlic. Season, cover with a lid and cook on a low heat for 15 minutes. Add the vinegar and sugar and cook for a further 5 minutes.

2 Melt the butter in a frying pan and fry the mushrooms. Season, add the thyme and cook for 3–4 minutes. Add a squeeze of lemon juice.

3 To serve, toast the brioche, place a slice on a plate, spread on a portion of cooked onions, top with the mushrooms and finish with shaved Parmesan.

Tip
When you buy wild mushrooms, they're always full of dirt and grit. It's important to wash them really well but, when you do, wash them quickly and never leave them in the water. Mushrooms are like sponges and will soak up the water, which will dilute the flavour.

'sensational'

Crisp puff pastry with sweet onion, mushrooms and parsley dressing

In the restaurant, I serve a smaller version of this recipe as a vegetarian canapé. The parsley dressing makes a quick, easy sauce for seafood or try adding a couple of spoonfuls on top of a lamb casserole to add acidity and freshness.

Serves 4

1 Wild Mushrooms and Caramelised Onions on Brioche recipe (previous page), but without the brioche

4 x 12 x 7 cm puff pastry rectangles, rolled to 0.25 cm thickness and kept in the fridge

Parmesan shavings, to serve

For the parsley dressing

20 g pine nuts

½ bunch fresh flat leaf parsley

½ bunch fresh basil

¼ bunch fresh mint

5 g freshly grated Parmesan

1 garlic clove

100 ml extra virgin olive oil

juice of ½ lemon

salt and freshly ground black pepper

1 Place the pine nuts in a dry frying pan and gently heat until they are toasted and golden brown. Keep to one side.

2 Preheat the oven to Gas Mark 4/180°C.

3 Cook the caramelised onions, following step 1 of the previous recipe. Place on a plate and leave to cool. Using a small knife, spread a thin layer of onions on to the puff pastry. This will be a lot easier to do if the pastry is cold. Place the pastry rectangles on a baking tray covered with baking parchment and cook in the oven for 10–12 minutes.

4 To make the parsley dressing, add all the ingredients except the seasoning to a blender and whizz. Season to taste.

5 Cook the wild mushrooms following step 2 of the previous recipe.

6 To serve, place a puff pastry tart on a plate, spoon on some mushrooms, add the parsley dressing and finish with Parmesan shavings.

sensational

'simple'

Fried courgettes with mint, tomatoes and almonds

This is a fast side dish for roast lamb or grilled fish. Courgettes are pretty good all year round so it's a recipe that will come in handy again and again.

Serves 4

50 ml olive oil

4 courgettes, sliced into 1 cm thick pieces

250 g cherry tomatoes, cut in half

½ red chilli, finely chopped

1 garlic clove, crushed

salt and freshly ground black pepper

20 g toasted flaked almonds

¼ bunch fresh mint, chopped

juice of ½ lemon

1 Pour the olive oil into a hot pan, add the courgettes and fry for 2 minutes until they start to brown.

2 Add the tomatoes, chilli and garlic, season and cook for a further 2 minutes.

3 Serve, finished off with the toasted flaked almonds, chopped mint and a squeeze of lemon juice.

SIMPLE

'sensational'

Stuffed courgette flowers with tomatoes and almonds

Courgette flowers are available during the summer months. You can stuff them with a number of different fillings. Try fresh crabmeat or smoked salmon mixed with cream cheese. If you can't find them, simply deep fry strips of courgettes and add a spoonful of the ricotta on top.

Serves 4

a sprig of fresh mint, finely chopped
120 g ricotta
salt and freshly ground black pepper
8 courgette flowers
sunflower or groundnut oil, for frying
a handful fresh herbs, to garnish

For the dressing

250 g cherry tomatoes, cut into quarters
1 garlic clove, crushed
½ red chilli, finely chopped
20 g toasted flaked almonds
1 shallot, finely chopped
20 ml balsamic vinegar
50 ml extra virgin olive oil
salt and freshly ground black pepper

For the batter

100 g self-raising flour
200 ml sparkling water

1 To make the dressing for the flowers, place the cherry tomatoes in a bowl, add the garlic, chilli, almonds, shallot, balsamic vinegar and olive oil. Season and mix well.

2 To make the stuffing for the courgette flowers, mix the mint in a bowl with the ricotta and a touch of seasoning. Spoon this mixture into a piping bag.

3 Carefully open the flowers and, using your fingers, remove the stems. Pipe the stuffing into the flowers, making sure the cheese is completely covered with the petals of the flower.

4 To make the batter, place the flour in a bowl, pour in the sparkling water and lightly mix with a fork. When making a batter for deep frying, don't try and make it completely smooth. Ideally you want a lumpy batter. These lumps will have pockets of air that will make the batter lighter.

5 Half fill a pan with oil and heat until a drop of batter sizzles and browns immediately on hitting the oil. If you have a deep fat fryer, heat it to 180°C. Dip the stuffed courgette flowers into the batter and deep fry for 3 minutes Take out, drain on kitchen paper and season.

6 Spoon the cherry tomatoes on to a plate and place two flowers on top. Garnish with fresh herbs and serve immediately.

sensational

see picture overleaf

Stuffed courgette flowers
are simple to make, but
look and taste amazing.

'sensational'

'simple'

Caramelised pears, chicory and grilled goat's cheese

Warm pears and goat's cheese, together with fresh chilled watercress and chicory, create a delicious combination of sweet, salty and bitter flavours with a contrast of hot and cold.

Serves 4

2 ripe pears, peeled, quatered
   and cored
20 g unsalted butter
1 teaspoon caster sugar
15 g walnuts
2 red chicory
½ bunch watercress
50 ml olive oil
1 tablespoon red wine vinegar
salt and freshly ground black pepper
4 x 50 g individual portions of
   goat's cheese

1 Cut the pear quarters in half lengthways. Melt the butter in a pan and add the pears. Cook for 2 minutes, add the sugar and walnuts and cook for a further 2 minutes. Remove from the heat and keep to one side.

2 Trim the root off the chicory and separate into individual leaves, then cut the leaves in half lengthways and place in a bowl. Add the watercress and dress with the olive oil and vinegar. Season.

3 Place the cheeses on a baking tray and place under a hot grill for 1 minute.

4 To serve, pile some watercress and chicory on a plate, place a goat's cheese on top and spoon on the pears and walnuts.

make it sensational

'sensational'

Crisp baked goat's cheese with pears and chicory

Have you ever brought a loaf of bread and not quite finished it before the last pieces start to go stale? Well, this recipe is a fantastic way of using up all those last slices. At Pearl I fill the goat's cheese with slices of truffle for a truly decadent experience.

Serves 4

8 slices white bread

2 medium free range egg yolks

1 Caramelised Pears, Chicory and Grilled Goat's Cheese recipe (previous page)

4 fresh basil leaves

100 g unsalted butter, melted

25 g black or white sesame seeds

Tip

Once the cheeses are wrapped and dipped in the melted butter, they will keep in the fridge for 3–4 days. Very handy for dinner parties if you're not sure whether there are any vegetarians. Instead of using a leaf of basil, try using sun-dried tomatoes or piquillo peppers.

Wrap the goat's cheese in bread and then bake until crispy (see step 3)

1 Preheat the oven to Gas Mark 6/200 °C.

2 Using a round cutter slightly larger than the goat's cheese, cut eight circles out of four of the slices of bread. With a rolling pin, roll out the other four slices of bread until thin. Cut off the crusts with a knife and cut each rolled square of bread into two equal sized rectangles.

3 To wrap each goat's cheese, use a pastry brush to brush one side of a bread circle and rectangle with egg yolk. Repeat with a second bread circle and rectangle. This will help to stick the bread on to the goat's cheese. Take a leaf of basil and place on top of a cheese. Put the two egg-washed circles of bread on the top and bottom of the cheese. Take one of the rectangles and wrap around the cheese with the egg-washed side touching the cheese. Use the other rectangle to completely encase the goat's cheese. They should overlap slightly – make sure it's well sealed. Dip in the melted butter and sprinkle the sesame seeds on top. Repeat the process with the other cheeses. Once they're all wrapped and dipped, place on a baking tray and cook for 10–12 minutes or until golden brown.

4 While the cheeses are baking in the oven, cook the caramelised pears and dress the chicory and watercress following steps 1 and 2 of the previous recipe. Serve immediately with the baked goat's cheeses.

see pictures overleaf

'simple'

'The crunchy toasted bread and sesame seeds
really set off the soft, tangy goat's cheese.'

'sensational'

'simple'

Peas, broad beans and sugar snaps

This dish works equally well with frozen peas and broad beans. It has to be the fastest way to serve spring vegetables. It's a perfect partner for steamed fish or barbecued lamb. Try adding some crispy fried bacon for a meaty alternative.

Serves 4
1 gem lettuce
25 g unsalted butter
100 g fresh peas
100 g fresh broad beans
100 g sugar snaps
100 ml vegetable stock (see Tip on page 26)
salt and freshly ground black pepper

1 Cut off the root of the gem lettuce and finely shred with a knife.

2 Melt the butter in a pan, add the peas, broad beans and sugar snaps and cook for 2 minutes. Add the stock, season and cook for a further 2 minutes. Finally add the lettuce and serve immediately.

Tip
When cooking with fresh broad beans, take them out of the pods, quickly blanch by placing them in boiling water for 10 seconds, then plunge them into iced water. Now carefully slip off the skins.

SIMPLE

'sensational'

Spring vegetables 'en papillote'

'En papillote' means 'in a parcel'. Normally it's a method used for cooking seafood, but cooking vegetables this way is different and delicious. You don't lose any of the goodness of the vegetables and the flavours combine to make a tasty dish. Come up with your own combination, just remember that all the ingredients you add to the parcel have to cook in around the same time. Also, think carefully about the combination of the flavours. Apart from that, be creative!

Serves 4
12 baby carrots, scraped clean
8 baby leeks
100 g fresh peas
100 g fresh broad beans
40 g sugar snaps
a sprig of fresh tarragon
20 g unsalted butter
salt and freshly ground black pepper
juice of 1 lemon
120 ml vegetable stock (see Tip on
    page 26)

1 Preheat the oven to Gas Mark 6/200°C.

2 Cut four squares of baking parchment, 25 x 25 cm. Divide the vegetables into four and carefully place one portion in the centre of each baking parchment. Add a quarter of the tarragon and butter to each. Season. Gather up the edges before adding a squeeze of lemon juice and a quarter of the stock to each. Tie the edges with string to make parcels. Place on a baking tray and bake in the oven for 15 minutes.

3 To serve, either cut open with a pair of scissors and place in a bowl or serve as they are.

'simple'

Honey roasted root vegetables

Whenever I cook Sunday lunch at home (which isn't very often) I always cook this recipe. The different colours of the honey glazed vegetables make for an appetising eye-full.

Serves 6

½ celeriac

2 medium carrots

2 parsnips

1 small swede

50 ml olive oil

salt and freshly ground black pepper

30 g unsalted butter

1 whole garlic clove

a sprig of fresh rosemary

a sprig of fresh thyme

2 tablespoons runny honey

1 Preheat the oven to Gas Mark 4/180°C.

2 Peel all the vegetables and cut them into 3 cm sized wedges.

3 Heat an ovenproof pan and add the olive oil. Wait until the oil is hot then add the vegetables. Cook for 5 minutes. Once they have started to caramelise, season and add the butter, garlic, rosemary and thyme. Mix well and place in the oven for 6 minutes.

4 Test to see if the vegetables are cooked by inserting a small knife into them. Remove the garlic, rosemary and thyme. Add the honey and coat well. Serve immediately.

Tip

A great tip when roasting vegetables or potatoes is to season them after they have turned golden brown. Salt draws the moisture out of vegetables and potatoes, so if you season them before they caramelise the moisture that is drawn out prevents them from colouring quickly and evenly. Ever had roast potatoes that stick to the pan? The same tip applies here – season them after they have started to turn a golden brown.

SIMPLE

see picture overleaf

'sensational'

Glazed root vegetables with star anise and cumin

Cooking and glazing vegetables with chicken stock maximises their flavour. Only a small quantity of stock is added to the vegetables. As they cook and the stock reduces, the flavours are intensified and the vegetables will become sticky and glazed. This is how I cook most of the vegetables in the restaurant.

Serves 4

1 Honey Roasted Root Vegetables recipe (previous page)

1 tablespoon cumin seeds

3 star anise

200 ml chicken or vegetable stock (see Tip on page 26)

1 Start to fry the vegetables in olive oil following the recipe on the previous page. Cook for 5 minutes until they start to caramelise. Season, then add the butter, garlic, rosemary, thyme plus cumin and star anise.

2 Cook for a further 2 minutes, then add the stock and reduce until the vegetables become sticky and shiny. If they are not quite cooked, add a little more stock. Add the honey and serve.

sensational

'simple'

The jewel-like colours
of the honey-glazed
vegetables brighten up
a Sunday roast.

'Aim for balance when you're deciding on a pudding – think about what has gone before and don't choose a heavy pudding to follow a filling main.'
Jun

Puddings

'simple'

Warm rich chocolate pudding

This dish is a guaranteed crowd pleaser. Remember, when buying chocolate you get what you pay for, so use the best quality chocolate you can afford.

Serves 4

unsalted butter, softened, for greasing

75 g plain flour, plus extra for flouring
    the ramekins

125 g unsalted butter, cut into 2.5 cm
    dice

170 g good quality dark chocolate
    (60–70% cocoa solids)

3 medium free range eggs

60 g caster sugar

icing sugar, for dusting

ice cream, to serve

Tip

If you're making the puddings for a dinner party, make them the day before and leave them in the fridge.

1 Using a pastry brush, apply a thin coating of butter to the inside of four medium ramekins (if you do not have ramekins, teacups will do). Cover the buttered insides with a light dusting of flour, tapping the sides and shaking out any excess flour. Place the ramekins in the fridge until required.

2 Place the diced butter and chocolate into a heatproof bowl and place the bowl on a pan filled with 6 cm of simmering water. Using a spatula, stir the chocolate and butter until they have both melted and mixed together. Remove the pan from the heat and leave to one side.

3 Break the eggs into a large bowl and add the caster sugar. Using an electric whisk on full speed, whisk them together for 5 minutes until they become light and fluffy and triple in size. (This is called a sabayon.)

4 Take half of the sabayon and, using a spatula, gently mix it into the chocolate and butter until completely combined. Repeat with the other half of the sabayon. Gradually add the flour to the mixture until completely incorporated.

5 Spoon the pudding mix equally into the floured ramekins and place in the fridge for 2 hours to set. Preheat the oven to Gas Mark 6/200°C.

6 Once set, place the puddings on a baking tray and put them in the oven for 6 minutes. Remove from the oven and allow to stand for 1 minute. Dust with icing sugar and serve immediately with a scoop of ice cream.

see picture overleaf

'sensational'

Chocolate fondant with cherry and mint compote

The English cherry season is short, so make the most of them when they're around. When they aren't available, try using raspberries or oranges instead.

Serves 4

1 Warm Rich Chocolate Pudding
   recipe (previous page)
ice cream, to serve
4 fresh mint tips
icing sugar, for dusting
For the cherry compote
20 g unsalted butter
400 g fresh cherries, pitted and
   cut in half
40 g caster sugar
juice of ½ lemon
finely grated zest of 1 unwaxed lemon
½ bunch fresh mint, finally shredded

1 To make the cherry compote, melt the butter in a pan on a medium heat. Add the cherries and cook for 2 minutes, stirring occasionally. Add the sugar, lemon juice and zest and simmer for 6–7 minutes. Remove from the heat and allow to cool. Add the shredded mint.

2 Make the Warm Rich Chocolate Pudding mixture, buttering and flouring the ramekins as before. Put the pudding mixture into a piping bag (see page 9) with a medium sized nozzle and half fill the ramekins. (If you don't have a piping bag, carefully spoon the mix into the ramekins.) Using the back of a spoon, make a small well in the centre of the pudding mix. Place a teaspoon of cherry compote into each well. Pipe the remaining pudding mix over the compote. Place the ramekins in the fridge for 2 hours to set.

3 Preheat the oven to Gas Mark 6/200°C.

4 Place the puddings on a baking tray and cook for 5 minutes. Remove from the oven and allow to stand for 1 minute. Place a plate upside down on top of each ramekin and turn both the plate and the ramekin over. Remove the ramekin.

5 To serve, place a couple of spoonfuls of cherry compote next to the fondant and finish with a ball of ice cream, a mint tip and a light dusting of icing sugar.

Tip
This compote makes a great topping for natural yoghurt, or blend it with milk for a tasty milkshake.

sensational

'simple'

Rhubarb crumble

You can't go wrong with a classic rhubarb crumble. Always try to use forced rhubarb, it's the best you can buy! It's in season from January to April. The long pink stems make a vibrant crumble.

Serves 4

For the poached rhubarb

500 g rhubarb, washed and cut into
    1.5 cm dice
200 g caster sugar
100 ml grenadine or Ribena
70 g fresh ginger, peeled and crushed

For the crumble

100 g plain flour
70 g ground almonds
1 teaspoon ground ginger
70 g caster sugar
70 g unsalted butter, cut into
    1 cm dice

1 First, poach the rhubarb. Place in a large bowl. Place 600 ml water, the sugar, grenadine or Ribena and ginger in a pan. Bring to the boil, remove from the heat and pour over the rhubarb. Cover the bowl with cling film several times, making it airtight. Leave for 20 minutes, then remove the rhubarb and set aside.

2 For the crumble, place the flour, ground almonds, ground ginger and sugar in a large bowl. Add the diced butter and, using your thumbs and fingers, rub the mixture together to create a breadcrumb-like mixture.

3 Preheat the oven to Gas Mark 3–4/170°C.

4 Place the rhubarb in a medium-sized ovenproof dish and cover with the crumble. Place in the oven and cook for 18–20 minutes until golden brown. Allow to stand for 10–15 minutes before serving.

Tip
Cooking the crumble mixture on its own (see next page) makes a great topping for ice cream, or you can mix it with yoghurt and berries for a delicious daytime treat.

SIMPLE

'sensational'

Chilled summer rhubarb crumble

I know it's tempting just to buy a packet of ready made custard but, believe me, home made custard with fresh vanilla is a world apart and, once you've mastered it, it's incredibly versatile.

Serves 4

1 x Poached Rhubarb recipe
  (previous page), but leaving the
  rhubarb whole
1 x Crumble recipe (previous page)
vanilla ice cream, to serve
For the crème anglaise (custard)
iced water
125 ml milk
125 ml double cream
1 vanilla pod, split and seeds
  removed and kept, or one drop of
  vanilla extract
5 medium free range egg yolks
45 g caster sugar

✳ Making the chilled summer
crumble in individual glasses
results in a more sophisticated
dessert. Cooking each element
of the dish separately and then
putting it together makes a
lighter crumble.

1 Preheat the oven to Gas Mark 3–4/170°C.

2 Make the poached rhubarb, but this time leave it in the liquid to cool down.

3 Make the crumble, but this time place on to a baking tray and cook in the oven for 15–20 minutes or until golden brown.

4 Place a sieve on top of a medium bowl and put this bowl into a larger bowl filled with iced water. Pour the milk and cream into a pan, add the vanilla seeds and pod and bring to the boil. While you wait for the milk to boil, whisk together the egg yolks and sugar. Pour the boiling milk on to the yolks, whisking continuously. Pour the mix back into the pan and place on a low heat. Using a wooden spoon, constantly stir the mixture until it turns glossy and is thick enough to coat the back of the spoon. Pour through the sieve into the medium iced bowl and allow to cool.

5 To serve, drain the rhubarb from its juice and remove the ginger. Take four glasses (about 125 ml in size) and add 3 tablespoons of custard to the bottom of each one. Cut the rhubarb into 8 cm pieces and divide equally between the glasses. Finish with a small ball of vanilla ice cream and top with crumble.

Variation
Try replacing the rhubarb with fresh berries and add a few drops of alcohol, such as amaretto, crème de cassis or whiskey.

'simple'

Cinnamon poached pears with chocolate sauce

These pears taste even better if they're poached the day before. Instead of cinnamon, try using different spices like star anise, cloves and vanilla.

Serves 4

For the poached pears

250 g caster sugar

500 ml white wine

250 g water

2 cinnamon sticks

finely grated zest and juice of ½ lemon

4 medium ripe pears (Conference are best), peeled

For the chocolate sauce

150 ml water

150 g caster sugar

50 g cocoa powder

1 To make a poaching liquid, place the sugar, wine, water, cinnamon sticks, lemon zest and lemon juice in a medium pan. Preferably using a melon-baller (see page 9), fully scoop out the core of each pear. Place the pears in the pan with the poaching liquid and cover with a circular sheet of baking paper. Place a medium sized plate on top of the paper to prevent the pears from floating. Place on the heat, bring to a simmer and cook for 4–5 minutes. Remove from the heat and allow to cool. Place in the fridge until needed.

2 For the chocolate sauce. pour the water and sugar into a pan and bring to the boil. Reduce the heat and add the cocoa powder, continuously whisking for 4–5 minutes. Pour the liquid through a sieve into a bowl and store in the fridge.

3 To serve, remove the pears from the poaching liquid and arrange them in a serving dish with the cinnamon sticks. Pour over the chocolate sauce.

Tip
For the colder months, warm the pears up in the liquid before serving. This works especially well if you replace the white wine with a red wine.

make it sensational

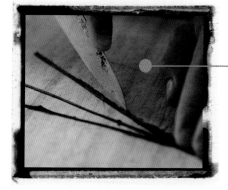

SIMPLE

'sensational'

Saffron poached pears with chocolate mousse

Saffron and pears might seem a strange combination, but trust me it works! You only need a pinch of saffron and the pears will take on the vivid yellow colour. Absolutely stunning!

Serves 4

1 Cinnamon Poached Pears with Chocolate Sauce recipe (previous page), but add a pinch of saffron threads and replace the white wine with 500 ml Sauternes

4 mint tips or 2 vanilla pods

For the chocolate mousse

200 g dark chocolate, finely chopped

80 ml milk

1 medium free range egg yolk

4 medium free range egg whites

20 g caster sugar

Slice a vanilla pod into a fan shape to add a funky touch to the saffron pear (see Tip)

1 Poach the pears, but add a pinch of saffron threads and replace the white wine with 500 ml Sauternes. Make the Chocolate Sauce.

2 For the chocolate mousse, place the chocolate into a large bowl. Pour the milk into a pan and bring to the boil. Whisk into the chocolate and add the egg yolk. Using an electric mixer, whisk the egg whites and sugar together in a bowl to form a stiff meringue. Take half the meringue and, using a spatula, fold it into the chocolate. Repeat with the other half. Pour the mousse into a container and place in the fridge for 2 hours to set.

3 To serve, remove the pears from the juice and sit them on kitchen paper to remove any excess liquid. Dip a spoon into the chocolate sauce and, holding a plate with one hand, flick the sauce on to the plate (do this over a sink). Place a pear on the middle of the plate. Take an ice cream scoop (use a spoon if you don't have an ice cream scoop) and dip it into hot water, then use it to make a ball of chocolate mousse. Place this next to the pear and garnish with a mint tip or vanilla pod (see Tip).

Tip

If you like, garnish with a vanilla pod. Split each pod lengthways in two. Remove the seeds. Cut along the halved length three times to form a branch. Repeat to make four branches. Place the pods on baking parchment and place in the oven at Gas Mark ¼/110°C until crisp.

see pictures overleaf

'simple'

'Poach a pear with a touch of saffron
for stunning colour and flavour.'

'sensational'

'sim<u>ple</u>'

Bread and butter pudding

A simple British classic. Serve this warm with vanilla ice cream or custard. The secret when cooking this pudding is to buy the best free range eggs that you can afford.

Serves 4

6 thick slices white bread

80 g unsalted butter, softened

100 g raisins or sultanas

For the custard mix

550 ml full-fat milk

550 ml double cream

2 medium free range egg yolks

8 medium free range eggs

200 g caster sugar

1 teaspoon vanilla extract

1 Butter the slices of bread evenly on one side. Cut in half diagonally and arrange them butter side up in a medium sized ovenproof dish (it should be able to hold 1.5 litres of liquid). Sprinkle the raisins or sultanas over the top.

2 Pour the milk, cream, yolks, eggs, sugar and vanilla extract into a bowl and lightly whisk. Pour through a fine sieve on to the buttered bread. Let the pudding stand for 30 minutes to allow the custard to soak into the bread.

3 Preheat the oven to Gas Mark 1/140°C.

4 Place a tea towel in a deep-sided baking tray and put the dish on top of the towel. Fill the baking tray with warm water until it comes three quarters of the way up the sides of the dish. Carefully place the tray in the oven and cook for 55–60 minutes. Remove the dish from the baking tray and allow to stand for 30 minutes before serving.

Tip

To give the pudding a shiny glaze, simply boil some apricot jam with a little water and, using a pastry brush, coat the top of the cooked pudding with the jam.

see picture overleaf

SIMPLE

'sensational'

Apricot and brioche spiced pudding

They say that you can't improve on a classic, but I really think that this one does. Using brioche gives a richer, more flavoursome pudding.

Serves 6

4 fresh apricots, stoned and diced, or
    12 dried apricots
400 g sliced brioche
100 g unsalted butter, softened
100 g raisins or sultanas
1 Custard Mix recipe (previous page)
1 teaspoon ground cinnamon
½ teaspoon allspice
finely grated zest of 2 oranges
seeds from 1 vanilla pod (see Tip on
    page 168)

1 Sprinkle an even layer of diced apricot into the bottom of an ovenproof dish. Butter the brioche and arrange butter side up over the apricot. Sprinkle the raisins or sultanas over the top.

2 Make the custard mix, adding the cinnamon, allspice, orange zest and vanilla seeds with the other ingredients for the custard mix. Whisk lightly. Pour through a sieve on to the brioche and allow the pudding to stand for 30 minutes.

3 Preheat the oven to Gas Mark 1/140°C.

4 Place a tea towel in a deep-sided baking tray and put the dish on top of the towel. Fill the baking tray with warm water until it comes three quarters of the way up the sides of the dish. Carefully place the tray in the oven and cook for 55–60 minutes. Remove the dish from the baking tray and allow to stand for 30 minutes before serving.

Variation
As an alternative, replace the brioche with panettone.

'simple'

"A classic pudding – simply delicious."

'simple'

Strawberry sherry trifle

You can't beat a proper trifle! There are so many bad versions that it has lost its appeal. But this one puts it back on the map.

Serves 4

400 g strawberries, topped and sliced

140 g caster sugar

**2 leaves of gelatin, soaked in
    iced water**

12 sponge fingers

100 ml sweet sherry

**6 strawberries, topped and cut
    into quarters**

400 ml double cream

**25 g amaretto or digestive biscuits,
    crushed**

For the custard

450 ml milk

1 teaspoon vanilla extract

50 g caster sugar

25 g cornflour

2 medium free range egg yolks

Tip If you're making this for young kids, simply replace the sherry with fruit juice and finish the trifle with jelly sweets and chocolate.

1 Place a sieve on top of a bowl and leave to one side. To make the custard, pour 400 ml of milk and the vanilla extract into a pan and bring to the boil. In a separate bowl, whisk together the sugar, cornflour and the remainder of the milk. Pour the boiling milk over the cornflour mix and whisk together. Pour back into the pan and place on a medium heat. Whisk continuously for 5 minutes or until the custard thickens. Pour though the sieve and whisk in the egg yolks. Place a layer of cling film on top of the custard to prevent a skin from forming and chill in the fridge.

2 Place the 400 g of sliced strawberries and 40 g of the caster sugar in a pan. Place on a medium heat and cook for 5 minutes or until the strawberries release their juices, stirring occasionally. Pour into a blender and purée.

3 Drain the gelatin from the iced water, giving it a good squeeze to remove any excess liquid. Add to the warm strawberry purée and stir until it completely dissolves.

4 Dip the sponge fingers into the sherry and place them in a medium-sized dish with the quartered strawberries.

5 Pour the strawberry purée on top of the sponge fingers and place the dish in the fridge to set. Once the jelly has set, pour over the cold custard and place back in the fridge for 30 minutes to allow the custard to reset.

6 Whisk together the cream and remaining sugar to a soft peak. Spoon on top of the custard and sprinkle with the crushed amaretto biscuits.

SIMPLE

'sensational'

Strawberry champagne trifle

You can't get more English than strawberries and champagne. This is a real summer pudding when strawberries arc at their best. For a cheaper option, try replacing the champagne with sparkling wine.

Serves 4

400 g strawberries, topped and sliced

40 g caster sugar

1 Custard recipe (previous page)

2 leaves of gelatin, soaked in
    iced water

100 ml champagne

8 sponge fingers

50 ml sweet sherry

4 strawberries, topped and quartered

25 g caster sugar

200 ml double cream

25 g amaretto biscuits, crushed

Tip The juice from the strawberries makes a refreshing chilled summer soup.

1 Place the strawberries in a heatproof bowl with the sugar and place on a pan of simmering water for about 1 ½ hours. The strawberries will release a lot of juice.

2 Make the Custard and chill in the fridge.

3 Place a fine sieve over a bowl and pour the strawberries into it, allowing all of the juice to drain into the bowl. Warm the juice in a pan over a low heat.

4 Remove the gelatin from the water, giving it a good squeeze to remove any excess liquid, and dissolve it in the warm strawberry juice. Pour this through a sieve into a bowl and place in the fridge until semi-set. This normally takes about 2 hours.

5 Whisk the champagne into the semi-set jelly and place to one side.

6 Dip two of the sponge fingers into the sherry and place them in the bottom of a champagne flute, along with four strawberry quarters. Repeat with three more champagne flutes. Divide the champagne jelly among the glass flutes and put them in the fridge until set.

7 Once set, remove the flutes from the fridge and spoon 2 tablespoons of cold custard on to the jelly, leaving a little space for the cream. Whisk together the sugar, cream and crushed amaretto biscuits until a soft peak forms, then spoon on top of each glass.

see picture overleaf

Champagne and strawberries
– summer in a glass.

sensational

Acknowledgements

I cannot believe that it has been almost three years since I first had the idea for this book. During this time I have come to recognise and appreciate the importance of certain people, whose support and patience have been invaluable.

I would like to thank all the chefs and front of house at Pearl for their continuing hard work and dedication. I would like to mention, in particular, Spencer Ralph for helping out over the months when I was writing and Benjamin Knell, my pastry chef, for giving up all those Sundays, testing and writing recipes.

For me, the most important part of a cookbook is the photography. When I envisaged this book I wanted the dishes to look enticing and beautiful, yet simple. Steve Lee has captured this perfectly and I want to express my sincere gratitude to him. To Lajos, Ben, Filippo and Greg, thank you for giving up your days off to help with the photo shoot.

Because it is my first book, I was a little apprehensive about the whole thing, but I was fortunate enough to have been assigned a fantastic editor – Paula Borton – who was understanding and supportive of the vision I had for the book, giving sound advice when needed. Thank you for everything.

I would also like to thank Borra, without whom there would not be a book. Finally, I want to thank Clementine Hancox for having patience with my weird system of hand delivering the recipes. The more I think about it the stranger it seems!

JT